MW00874764

Up:
A Love Letter to the Down Syndrome Community

Ashley Asti

Copyright © 2020 Ashley Asti

ISBN: 9798673862384

"Life gives us something that we could hardly imagine."
—Marcel Proust

ALSO BY ASHLEY ASTI

I Always Thought I Was Fire:
A Memoir Through the Elements

The Moon and Her Sisters

I Have Waited for You: Letters from Prison

Yoga Heartsongs

A Yoga Teacher's Guide to Creative Living

Your Nature is to Bloom

CONTENTS

Dear Reader,

I've called this book a "love letter," and while it is truly a book of stories, I like to keep my promises. So, dear reader, this is for you.

I pray that when you hold this book in your hands and gently open it to begin reading what's carried within its pages, that the fragrance of love greets you, no matter who you are and no matter what page you land on.

I pray that you feel these stories in your heart, that you greet them with wonder and surprise, with head-nodding and resonance and "Oh, I know that feeling too." Whether you have Down syndrome or not or whether you love someone with Down syndrome or not, I hope you feel a little less alone and a little more connected. A little more nourished.

I pray that you also greet all the unknown parts, the parts that aren't familiar to you, with gratitude. I believe curiosity is the beginning of empathy and when we're curious enough, that's when we finally take the time to really listen—to listen, even, to those who seem so unlike ourselves. May we appreciate what we learn from them.

I pray that you feel joy and uplift. This is not a book with only rainbows; these stories attest to the storms, too. The rains and the rainbows. Because, at the end of the day, these are human stories, Down syndrome just happens to be a part of them, a single thread drawing them together. Down syndrome is not all they are. These are stories of life lived in different shades, with fullness, with heart, through tragedy and back up, again. I hope, no matter what journeys they take you on, that each story leaves you a little more lifted than you were before. A little *up*, if you will.

Because when children are brought into the world with an extra chromosome—with Down syndrome, that is—the first words parents often hear are, "I'm sorry," as if Down syndrome itself is something to be down about. It's not. I want to say, "Congratulations." I want to say, "What a beautiful gift you've brought into the world, one more being here for a reason, here with purpose." I want to say, "Oh, mama," or "Oh, dad—this new little being is going to lift you up."

There will be challenges along the way, sure. We all have them; that is a human phenomenon, not a Down syndrome one. But life is precious—wild, unexpected, and precious—and I want you to savor all of it, the whole ride.

For the past few months, as I've begun to tell people that I'm writing this book, they've asked me, "Oh, is it for new parents of babies with Down syndrome? Are you writing it to give them hope?" Dear reader, if you're a new parent of a baby with Down syndrome, I pray you find hope in these pages. That you see the blessings of the life that awaits you and your child somewhere in these words. I hope this book honors you. I hope, somehow, that it tells a piece of your story, too, even if only a small piece, a glimmer. I hope you and your family and your new little blessing build your own story and come back to share it with me or with the world. There is nothing more needed in the world than each of us being exactly who we are, shining our light exactly as we are.

But I've written this book as a celebration of a community that has moved me, changed me, helped me bloom; it's for anyone. I don't have a sibling or a child or an aunt with Down syndrome. I am blessed to call myself one of "the lucky few" because I've been brought into this community by friendship. I am friends with Brittany Schiavone, a creative and charismatic and knows-what-she-wants kind of woman who happens to have Down syndrome, and I wonder often how I got so lucky.

I wrote this book because Brittany Schiavone is the founder of Brittany's Baskets of Hope, a nonprofit that provides resources, hope, and love to families of new babies with Down syndrome across the United States and I happen to serve on its Board of

Directors. Each month, we send out dozens of welcome "baskets of hope" to families that began just like Brittany's because we know that everyone's arrival in this world, no matter who you are or how you're born, deserves to be celebrated.

I wrote this book because, through Brittany's Baskets of Hope, I have gotten the chance to hear about the lives of people with Down syndrome all across the country. I have been sent photos and stories and messages, and I have gotten to meet them in person. It has opened my world, offering me a sense of connection and faith I didn't know I needed before.

This book tells six stories, each one tied together with the thread of Down syndrome. But I hope you don't see them as *Down syndrome stories*. I hope you see them as they are, stories of people. I have written about The Joyful Artist, a man with Down syndrome who creates visionary abstract paintings in his studio in Dallas, Texas. About The Dreamer, a yogi and mom of four in New Jersey; one of those four was born with Down syndrome just a few months ago. About The Peacemaking Mama, a mom who is raising her children with intention, including her little girl with Down syndrome whom she and her husband adopted four years ago. I've written about The Beauty, a model with Down syndrome who knows that true beauty is beauty of the heart; our radiance comes from within. I've written about The Dancing Dad, who used his dancing gifts to help his son through a medical journey. And, lastly, I've written about me. Not just me, but me and Brittany and the way our friendship has changed us both, has lifted us *up*.

I tried to tell stories of people of different colors, faiths, ages, places, and ways of being. But, of course, these six stories are only a shade of the whole Down syndrome community. We are all unique and one book can never capture it all.

This book is small, but I pray it is mighty. I pray it is mighty not because of what I have written, but because of the people who have filled it, the ones who took the time to sit with me and tell me their stories. Who were willing to be vulnerable and open. Who let me peek into their lives and their families all to spread a little something special to you, dear reader. A little bit of their personal magic that transcends them and, I hope, reaches us all. Because they have shared with their hearts, I hope that it touches something in your heart, too.

Dear reader, this is a love letter because there is no better word to describe what this unexpected adventure in my life—into a nonprofit and a friendship and a community—has done for me. It has shown me love.

And love is everything.

With gratitude,
Ashley

*How we come into this world,
how we are ushered in, met,
and hopefully embraced upon
arrival, impacts the whole of
our time on earth.*

—Alice Walker

*

What God intended for you goes far beyond anything you can imagine.

—Oprah Winfrey

*

The Joyful Artist

*Charlie French is an abstract painter based in Dallas, Texas.
He's nearing thirty and happens to have Down syndrome.*

What I remember most about talking to Charlie for
the first time one July day is his smile and his eyes.
His eyes seemed curious. Like he was present with
me, taking me and the experience of us talking in, and
yet like there was something else happening in his
own world, like a rich inner life I couldn't quite see
was hiding behind his eyes.

And that smile—wide, playful, a little enigmatic.

I was nervous even before the interview started and
when I sat down to talk with him and saw that smile
for the first time outside of photos, I said, "You
know, Charlie, I was a little nervous to talk to you
today and I was wondering why. And then I realized
it's because you're a bit of a celebrity, you're kind of a
big deal!" He and his mom laughed.

"Are you a celebrity, Charlie?" she said to him. And
there it was, again, just a flash of his smile.

As a writer, I love talking to artists of all kinds
because while our mediums may be different, while
Charlie speaks in colors on canvas and I speak in

words on pages, there's a delightful communion between us: there's something about hearing another artist's story that makes me nod my head and think, "Aha, yes, I know that feeling. I recognize something in you."

*

My crush on Charlie's art, which made me nervous before his interview, didn't begin that day with his curious eyes and his smile, but months before when I first discovered his art on Instagram.

His colors are vibrant; I love the oceans of blue. I love the flashes of red, sometimes just found in a small corner of his painting—almost hiding, but too bold to get lost. And then there are those shades of pink—fuchsia, magenta, bubble gum. There are lots of squares and shapes, sometimes intentional drips run down the painting, drawing your eye from symmetry to something wilder and freer, something more guttural or emotive. Maybe it feels like tears, maybe it feels like freedom, maybe it feels like rain calling to you, making itself present.

His art feels so vital, like it's living. Like the man who created it was deeply present; you can feel him in his paintings, unleashing himself. "Painting makes me feel happy," he told me. "Free and happy." With an abstract style, he has created paintings about the monkeys and sun and beach in Costa Rica, about ice cream and bubble gum, which makes him laugh. He has art about hope and joy, about oceans, and even about veggie burgers. "We're keeping it real," his mom laughed when I asked him what inspires his art and he included "food" in the list. I would later learn that chips and salsa are his favorite—he took a break from our interview to go grab some—"he's got priorities," his mom, Karen, laughed. And then Charlie added, "And sometimes I like guacamole."

"Oh, I love avocados!" I said as he sat back down from getting his chips and salsa. "I'm always up for guacamole."

But what moves me most about his work is the way he experiences the process. "Can you tell me a little more about what 'free' means to you, the way you say you use your imagination to be free?" I asked him.

"Just letting go," he said, and as he said it, he almost whisked away the air in front of him, brushing his hands through the air and releasing his fingers out to the sides. That's what free means to him. "It's joyful, sometimes," he said. "Sometimes, it's laughing…just let go."

*

I was talking recently to my friend Heather, who is a classically trained painter and a photojournalist. We were trading stories about what it feels like to come to the end of any creative project. She had recently embarked on a project where she collected photos of people over Zoom, a nod to the moment—it was May 2020 and a pandemic was raging. "Once the gathering work is done," she told me, once the real heat of creativity is over, and you're left on your own to complete it, to take those last final steps to bring it out into the world, it feels like "the party is over. Like everyone has gone home and you're left with just you and it.

"And that's when the critical voice comes in," she said. You have to face your work, to see it, to reckon with it, to wonder "whether it's good enough, whether anyone will want it."

I nodded my head. "It's at that point in the process where I sometimes let doubt in," I added. "I hate reading proofs of my books," I told her, because once it's set down on the page and I'm left with just it and me, I start criticizing it, doubting myself. Doubting my own creation."

And that's when I decided to tell her about Charlie.

*

For many artists, I think the deliciousness is the process. But so many of us place our art in the context of money or being worthy—will anyone pick up what we're putting down? Will our art be loved, needed, praised? Will we be able to make a living creating what we love? And so we let all these fears enter. But it's as if Charlie is creating in a space without these fears—it is pure love for him. Pure joy. He paints because he is an artist. Because he enjoys the process. Because selling a painting is about sharing joy. When I asked him what it feels like to sell a painting, I expected him to talk about money or excitement or fame. Instead, he just said, "It's good. I like to see people happy."

"You do like to see people happy, don't you?" his mom said to him. Turning to me, she added, "Charlie's not really about the money or fame. He doesn't have any desire for it…he feels good to get positive reinforcement, to see people happy, to get to enjoy his art. It's more experiential."

It's as if he has found a way to savor being *in it*, in the flow, and to live there as often as he can. No unnecessary ego distractions, no fear. He's not worried whether his art is wanted or needed or whether he's worthy. He does it for the love. *Just let go.*

*

But this doesn't mean he only knows joy. That he only knows lightness. His art comes from what I like to call The Deep, the center of him. The Deep is within us and our mission in life, I believe, is not to rise up to the top, to reach the summits of the world, but to dive deeper within us. Because *in* is not a cage; *in* is infinite; expansive. Everything we need to create begins within us.

Charlie seems to create from there.

When Charlie was 16, he got really sick and received a secondary diagnosis: Regression Disorder. His mom Karen told me, "Now there are Facebook groups for it, support groups. But it's only really come to light in the past few years. Back when he was 16, we had no idea what was going on." She continued, "It's pretty much a complete loss of skills. So art was really started therapeutically, to get back on track, to get the brain moving, to open expression."

Charlie's now 29. At 16, as he began the long journey to recovery, he was just doing art here and there —"we weren't painting a lot," Karen said. "We used it as a tool." But about six years ago, he began painting more. The thing is, his mom told me, at the time, "he painted in a lot of dark, dark colors."

But she remembers the moment something shifted: "We had just moved back to London," she said, "and within a couple of months, Charlie started to pick up yellow. I have his very first painting that he painted with a lot of dark colors, but there was this one small square of yellow"—and here she got choked up for a moment. "And I have it at my desk, still. Because that was all of a sudden—the shift."

At the time, he had been exploring different places to work. "We were living in London," his mom said, "and Charlie had been going to senior centers and different places doing volunteer work to see what he could do professionally. But he disliked it. Intensely. And he really loved painting."

So finally, after all those years working to move from darkness and to rediscover the light, about 18 months after he first painted with that spark of yellow, that little nod to his own awakening, Charlie came to her and said, "No more jobs. My job is an artist…Art for dollars."

That's when he declared himself an artist. That's when he knew, from The Deep of him, who he was.

*

Charlie didn't articulate this to me. He didn't call the place his work comes from "The Deep." He didn't tell me the story of his journey from dark to light; his mom shared it with me as he listened. But I am certain he knows it, that it lives within him. That he has experienced an artist's journey, or a "hero's journey."

Joseph Campbell came up with that last phrase—a hero's journey. It essentially means that the leaders, the artists, the visionaries among us, they don't just rise into the challenge and the role of being leaders and artists and visionaries. They must first go on a quest to find themselves. An inner journey. And this journey is often not easy. It's often dark and unclear —there's often pain and struggle and uncertainty along the way. Until, one day, they reach clarity. Until one day, they have reached a summit; they have discovered some revelation, some insight, something needed in the world. They are ready.

This means they can't stay out there on their quest any longer, at the pinnacle. They must come back. They must come back to serve, to give what they've learned, what they've got—as leaders or artists or visionaries. This is not the time to go it alone, to stay at the heights of the mountaintop; this is the time to return to share their wisdom.

Perhaps this is what Charlie did. He went out there on that quest, a journey where he lost the skills of who he once was. And so he painted in darkness.

But, one day, he reached the light, the summit, and for the first time in a long time, he was ready to bring in a dash of yellow—just a hint. But it was enough, enough to signal a change. His mom felt this in her heart as only a mother can.

And that's when he had to come back, come back to himself and to all of us. That's when it was time: he was an artist. It was time for him to share his art with the world. It was time for him, through his work, to show us his freedom and what creating freely means. To show us his joy and to share that joy with each of us who gets to gaze at his work or let it blaze brightly on the walls of our homes. To inspire us, to make us laugh. To invoke our curiosity. Because isn't that what good art does—it makes us curious? It provokes us. In this way, we become a part of it. What Charlie puts out in the world is no longer *just* his own; it becomes ours, too. We gather pieces of it within us and go off and create with them in our own lives. Our lives are collections of what we see, what we experience, who we meet.

Inspiration everywhere.

*

The black moment is the moment when the real message of transformation is going to come. At the darkest moment comes the light.

—Joseph Campbell

*

Today, Charlie paints in a bright and airy studio in Dallas, Texas. "It's in a cottage," Karen told me. We had been talking over Zoom, and that's when Charlie and his mom picked up the computer and turned it to face the sliding glass doors. Just beyond the doors, I could see sunshine raying down onto a bright aqua pool and, just beyond the pool, Charlie's house. "I like to listen to the water fountain in the pool," he told me. It inspires his imagination. (When I later asked him what else he likes to listen to while he works, he added, *The Little Mermaid* and The Three Tenors, although Charlie prefers to call them, "The Three Men." "He likes wordplay," his mom added.)

"Do you have anyone else in the studio with you when you paint?" I asked.

"My mom," he said, "who's the studio manager."

"I have a background in special ed, but I'm not an artist," she laughed.

"And Percy," Charlie added, referring to his dog whose official name is Percival French. "He sleeps on the floor. He's my assistant." (His other dog, Finn, I'm told, "is not an art fan. He likes to be on the couch and watch Netflix." Oh, a dog's life.)

The art Charlie creates in his studio is sold online and in galleries. "See, you're kind of a big deal," I said with a smile. "When you were a little kid, did you ever imagine this—that you'd be living this life as a painter with so many followers?"

In one single word, he put all my own existential doubt about being an artist to shame: "Yes," he said.

"No modesty here!" Karen laughed.

"We could all learn from that," I said. "What about you, Karen, did you always imagine this?"

"No, no. Charlie's always loved words. He read from a very early age, wrote a lot of creative stories, so I knew his imagination was really fun and interesting—but, art? No, it just never occurred to me. Charlie used to dress up like his dad with a tie and he wanted to go to school like that, all dressed up. So I thought maybe in an office? But we, with all our kids, are just like, *as long as you get up and do what you love in life…*"

When, later, Charlie got up to get chips and salsa, I would learn from his mom that Charlie's younger brother is a writer and his younger sister an actress. "Wow," I would remark, "you and your husband clearly made your children feel safe and comfortable to pursue their creativity."

"My husband and I are *not* artistic," Karen laughed. "And my husband feels the pressure…how are they going to survive?"

I laughed, too. "I get that. I have a dad."

*

If you visit Charlie's website or Instagram page, you'll see that it's called "Just Charlie French." He explained to me, "I am first Charlie French. Yes, I have Down syndrome, but I don't want to talk about that. I don't want you to see that. I want you to see me, Charlie French. Just Charlie French. Then I want you to see my art."

When Charlie was 11 or 12, his family was living in Austin and they had just been to the annual Buddy Walk, a big, community-wide event that celebrates the Down syndrome community. He and his family were very involved in the Down syndrome community and they had walked with a big group of friends from school and their families. "It was beautiful," his mom told me. But as they were leaving the walk that day, Charlie pulled his mom aside and said, "That's it. I'm done. There's no more Down syndrome. It's just me, Charlie French."

"He just kind of got in the car after that," his mom told me, "and I still remember so vividly standing in the parking lot and thinking, *Where do I go from here? What do I do?*"

Karen was certain that she needed to listen—"I have to hear him," she said. "That's the first thing I realized I needed to do. I needed to put away all my expectations, as parents have with their children, you know? And let that go. And that's pretty much been his consistent message since then. I really admire him for that."

*

Perhaps this is why Charlie's art is so heartfelt. Because he has created space for himself to be seen as who he is—Charlie, who as he tells me, is "an artist, a funny guy, diligent." We don't buy his art *because* he has Down syndrome. He's not an artist who's good, *you know, for a man with Down syndrome.* There is no pity or sense of being "special." Charlie is Charlie. He's talented and creative. We come to his canvases as they are.

And maybe that's because he comes to his canvases as he is, too.

"I think one of the really cool things about Charlie," Karen told me, "is that he doesn't shy away from a blank canvas. I've talked to a lot of artists before and that is a major hurdle." But as Charlie says, he can *just let go.* Every blank canvas is an adventure and you never know what it's going to become.

This is what is so surprising about Charlie—his ability to unleash himself. To approach a blank canvas before him not with fear or dread—not with worry over whether what he places down on that canvas will be brilliant enough. Innovative enough. Praised and wanted enough.

For Charlie, every blank canvas is an invitation—and he walks right up to it and says, *Yes.*

And in saying *yes* to every empty canvas, to the uncertainty ahead, a new exploration begins.

It's never been about the destination. Life is always fullest when you allow yourself to soak up every moment, exactly as it is. Let it delight you, surprise you, challenge you, change you.

Yes, it's always been about the journey.

*

When we finished up our conversation, I asked Charlie if there was anything else he'd like to share. "I like to invite people to my studio to paint with me," he said.

"He really does like when people come visit," Karen said. He likes the experience of community and joining together on a single giant canvas to create one work of art out of many.

The three of us had been talking virtually, over Zoom. "After this pandemic," I said, "I would love to visit…although I don't know if I could paint!" I laughed.

"Don't worry," Karen said. "Charlie will give you instructions. He'll turn on the music…it'll be fun."

"And maybe we could share some guacamole?" I asked.

Charlie French looked up at me and smiled.

*

If you ask me what I came to do in this world, I, an artist, will answer you: I am here to live out loud.

—Émile Zola

*

The Dreamer

Taryn Lagonigro is a yoga studio owner and mom to four girls, including a new baby with Down syndrome.

"Teaching yoga to these people in tiny boxes is definitely strange," Taryn said.

I laughed and agreed. "Right? It's so much harder to feel their energy."

Taryn and I began our conversation like two yoga teachers chatting (I'm a yoga teacher, too), chatting about what's it been like to teach yoga online via Zoom during a pandemic.

"I just started teaching yoga again last week for the first time during all this," she said, "because, coincidentally, I went on maternity leave at the same time the pandemic hit." It was early July when we spoke.

"Wow. Can you remind me how old Rhea is?" And here I double-checked that I was pronouncing her newest daughter's name right. It's pronounced like *Ray-ah*, like a ray from the sun, I thought as she told me.

"Rhea is 3 ½ months old now. Born March 29th. It's crazy. It's hard to keep track of days. And because she had heart surgery at two months old, I feel like that was a second birthday. So I feel like she's just a month old."

For a moment, I tried to imagine it all. What a little warrior Rhea must be—just two months in the world when a surgeon opens her heart. And here she is, going on, thriving. At just two months, she faced an obstacle many of us will never have to face in our lives, and she's still here, challenge accepted and summited. Perhaps she doesn't know this yet and this wasn't her choice, of course; maybe she didn't know what was ahead when they brought her into the operating room that day, but her body has lived through it. That is a strong girl.

At this point, I asked Taryn about what it was like to give birth during a pandemic—"I know this is not what our conversation today is really about," I said, "but I'm curious."

Because I am not a mother and have never had to juggle childcare, she explained added stresses I wouldn't have even considered before. In New Jersey, where Taryn lives, they went on lockdown "around March 13," she said. And she was hearing that hospitals weren't letting spouses or partners be there with the mothers giving birth. "So, everyday, I checked the visitor policy on the hospital's website," she told me. Fortunately, her husband was able to be there with her, but he couldn't stay. It was at the apex of the pandemic in the Northeast, they were supposed to be social distancing—no one except immediate family coming into contact with each other. So her husband didn't stay because they had, as she told me, "such a limited number of people who could help with the kids at home because of the quarantine."

"Ah, right, your other children," I interjected, still surprised by how much I didn't know about the demands of motherhood. Taryn has three older daughters—Sofia, Layla, and Genevieve, all under ten.

Taryn had done this three times before, so she knew the usual process, the celebrations and family gatherings that often accompany birth. "It was weird not having visitors come see me in the hospital," she told me. "But the hospital itself was so calm, and I was expecting a crazy situation. It was very quiet and the nurses were like, *We're fine*," as if saying, *In maternity, we've got this. This is nothing new. We're used to upheaval in the world, new lives crying and shouting as they make their way into this life.* God bless the nurses who help usher our babies into the world.

"Did you have to wear a mask?" I asked her.

"I did! I had to wear a mask during labor."

Again, astonished by her, I exclaimed, "You gave birth to a human being wearing a mask!"

She laughed and we both agreed that if she can do that, anyone else can wear a mask for ten minutes at the store. But I digress.

*

When Taryn was still pregnant and she received Rhea's diagnosis, she started a blog called "Our Journey Up." Down syndrome is named after the doctor—John Langdon Down—who first fully described the syndrome. But many people in the community have taken to flipping that word "Down" on its head. Again, while the name's origins don't stem from anything inherently negative, we like to see entering the Down syndrome community not as something that brings you down, but lifts you up. So Taryn's blog was aptly named to describe a journey into something new—*up* not down.

Taryn is a beautiful writer. She seems to express herself effortlessly, "from a heart place," I told her.

"I guess writing is a remembered passion for me," she said. "I always liked writing, maybe I just didn't have anything to write about for a little while."

I paused after she said that because it reminded me of the ways our voices seem to rise and fall in us, the ways we sometimes don't realize that our voice is there, in us. Not until something unexpected prompts it to rise in us, again, and we finally see it: it has been there all along. Perhaps that's the mystery of life— maybe we're always being directed toward a future we hadn't anticipated but that has been waiting for us, waiting for us to rise into it and, once we're there, it'll call on all our gifts.

Or maybe it is random. Either way, Taryn found a lost piece of herself after Rhea's diagnosis, calling on the words that had been hidden in her for a while, inviting in that remembered passion.

"I feel like, with writing," she said, "I've been finding therapy in putting all that stuff out there," and here she was referring to everything she has experienced as she makes her way through this unexpected diagnosis and life shift. I think the ways she expresses herself so honestly and with such heart makes it therapy not only for her, but for other people reading it, too, who can connect to it.

This is something Taryn knows deeply—the power of connection. When she first received Rhea's diagnosis, the genetic counselor immediately said, "What do you want to do?" as if her baby was no longer as valuable or wanted or needed in the world. And this is a very personal decision that every mother and her partner should be able to make privately about any pregnancy. But I wish doctors delivered the message better. "It's 2020," Taryn said, "and the message is still delivered in not necessarily the right way," often focusing on all the negatives or with sympathy.

"When we first got Rhea's diagnosis," she explained, "people didn't know what to say. Of course, our immediate family was like, *We love her no matter what.* But no one knew what to say and everyone seemed to be offering a lot of sympathy…And, you know, a year ago, if someone in my life said to me, *The baby I'm carrying is going to have Down syndrome,* I probably would have reacted with sympathy because I didn't know. I hadn't been in those shoes before. Now I know. I would say, *Congratulations!* Or *Everything's going to be fine.*"

This is the power of the Down syndrome community. If you Google "Down syndrome," you may find a lot of misinformation. But in the last few years as social media has risen to prominence in our culture, the Down syndrome community has found a fierce and loving home there, too—connections across space. Taryn began turning to this online community, people who have walked this path before her, for advice and information. But, it turns out, it wasn't advice she needed most: what she came to see is that hope was the most important resource.

"When I finally turned to the Down syndrome community, to others who have a family member with Down syndrome, their first reaction was always, *Congratulations!* And their first reaction was joy. Having that, it felt like I got a big, giant hug from all these strangers who were like, *Everything's going to be okay.*"

I'm the Social Media Director of Brittany's Baskets of Hope and, daily, I post photos of babies with Down syndrome on our social media pages. And what continues to surprise and delight me, nearly four years later, is that perfect strangers from across the country and around the globe comment. They leave messages of joy and hope and love for babies and their parents whom they've never met and probably never will. Parents of children with Down syndrome who are grown, whose children are 25 now, will write to the new parents and tell them this will be the best journey of their lives. Others remind the baby to "set your sights high, you can achieve anything." When babies are struggling in the NICU or undergoing surgery or battling just to keep going, these strangers will send prayers and love and healing wishes. They'll add these babies to their prayer lists at church or will include them in their daily meditations. I don't know how to describe it other than *nourishing*. Other than continually moving. Every day, I am delighted and surprised by kindness, by strangers welcoming in these new parents and saying, "You are not alone. I'm with you," even if you're far away.

Community matters.

Hope buoys us.

We need each other. We are all connected.

*

When the world told the caterpillar its life was over, the butterfly objected, "My life has just begun."

—Matshona Dhliwayo

*

At Brittany's Baskets of Hope, when we welcome a new child with Down syndrome into the world, we don't say, "I'm sorry." Because this moment, of ushering in new life, is a celebration! No matter who you are or how you're born, your arrival deserves to be celebrated.

But I don't ever want to pretend that the journey after hearing that diagnosis is always easy, that it is always full of joy and sunshine. Because, the truth is, I believe every parent needs to grieve in their own ways. Not because the child they have been given, a radiant new being who happens to have Down syndrome, is wrong or imperfect. But because their expectations have to shift.

Whether we admit to it or not, we all have expectations for ourselves, for our families, for how we think our lives should play out. And, so, I wanted to know: what did grief look like for Taryn? What did it feel like in her? Because grief is natural. But when Taryn wrote about her grief on her blog, she also wrote about something else, what she called her "new vision."

I found those two words compelling. I often use the word "vision" as if it is a mighty word, a word of transformation, of manifestation, of power. And Taryn took that same word and applied it to what some people would call a *hurdle* or a *challenge,* to what some people were offering her sympathy for and saying *I'm sorry* about.

When the genetic counselor first reached out to Taryn to deliver unsettling news, she wasn't certain it was Down syndrome, just that there was some "chromosomal abnormality," something potentially wrong, possibly something big. And, so, for a few days, she and her husband had to wait in that, in the unknown of what their daughter's life would be. In those few days, she realized this: "I think what that diagnosis did, or waiting on it, when I talk about my change in vision, I feel like I was focusing on all the wrong things for a while." She and her husband hadn't expected a fourth child and she laughed and thought, "It's 2020. Who has 4 children these days?" So when she first found out she was pregnant, before the Down syndrome diagnosis came and shifted their world, she teases that she was slightly embarrassed about even talking about the pregnancy—again, she worried people would wonder why she was having all these kids in 2020. That it was impractical. She wrote, "Will people even invite us over anymore? How do you even fly with a family of six? And suddenly everything about our house was bothering us." Would there be enough room in their still-needed-to-be-renovated home? And, so, at first, she and her husband, Raff, were just focused on the "craziness" of life, as she called it.

She described it like this:

At the time, I thought, "I have three kids, am a full time Vice President in corporate America, and a part time but kinda full time co-owner of a growing yoga studio. I was launching a teacher training program in four months, drowning in mountains of home organization projects, and had a to do list that only gets longer. I love babies, but having a fourth one wasn't totally in the plans at the moment. When I told Raff later that day [that she was pregnant], he was flooded with the same overwhelmed feelings.

"Our heads were spinning."

She told me, "We spent so much time in those first 13 weeks of my pregnancy focusing on *let's do this, let's do that…who's playing softball? Who's playing soccer?*"

But when the genetic counselor called for the first time and said something was almost certainly wrong, they suddenly found themselves spun in a whole other direction and, almost as if forced by nature, they began to re-see their worries in a new light. "We realized that all that stuff we were worrying about, all the negative things about having a fourth child, at the end of the day, it doesn't matter. It gave us perspective. When you realize you're going to have a child who maybe will, maybe won't do certain things that you put in your bucket of importance in your life, you kind of just shift your focus and think, at the end of the day, let's just make sure we have happy kids."

In fact, when they got that call, Taryn realized something even more precious: "Suddenly, when we had the possibility of not having her, meaning because something was wrong with the pregnancy, that maybe she wouldn't make it, she was all we wanted. So it really just jump-started that new vision, that focus on having a happy family, regardless of everything else."

Yes, at the end of the day, maybe what we should dream for is joy. For a happy life, a full life. For safety and connection and love.

*

What amazed me, though, is how quickly Taryn was able to set herself and her family on this new path, toward this new vision.

Beginning when I was in college, I spent years fighting the unfolding of my own life, doubting it, getting angry at it, insisting that it wasn't what I planned, not what I thought my life would be. Getting angry or frustrated didn't help me, it just sunk me deeper. And it took years for me to realize—instead of fighting life, instead of fighting the ways my life showed up at my metaphorical door, what if I softened? What if, like water, I trusted and went with the flow? What if I let my life be a conversation with the universe—maybe these weren't my original plans, but how could I embrace them? How could I re-see them as just as mighty and divine? In other words, how could I make the best out of my one wild and precious life, exactly as it was?

Carrying that in me, having lived it, made me curious. So I asked Taryn, "When you were stepping into your new vision, when you let yourself grieve a little, but then you chose to step into this new way of seeing your life, this new path, did you realize you were being courageous in that moment? Or was it just an innate thing, like something was calling you from within, calling you forward into it? I'm curious how you found acceptance, because I think so many of us struggle with that in our lives, Down syndrome diagnosis or not."

She looked at me and smiled. "I think that's where yoga comes in."

*

Taryn had practiced yoga on and off over the years, and she always found it relaxing and enjoyable. But, she told me, "After I had my second daughter, I didn't really have anything that was my own anymore." At the time, she was working full-time, adjusting to being a mom of two, and running back and forth between daycare drop-offs. There was no room for just her, she thought. "I was just kind of going through the motions."

She was just going through the motions until, one day, she realized she needed to do something. This wasn't working for her. A new yoga studio had just opened about a block or so from her home and she felt like it was a sign. *Just go take a yoga class*, the studio beckoned to her. So she did.

"It was a lightbulb moment for me," she said about that first class at the studio up the block. "Because, for an hour, I wasn't stressing about the thousand things you stress about being a new mom. So I started to get addicted to the feeling of hitting pause on my brain—and it was the only place where I did that, where I was able to hit pause and find that."

When she says, "find that," I think she means the quiet. Because what yoga beckons us to do is get quiet. And I don't just mean not talking during class; I mean it invites us into ourselves. It reminds us to get cozy and find some room within. To really listen, not

44

to the thousand things racing through our minds, but to begin, even if ever so slowly, to dive down a little deeper, from our heads into our hearts. That's where true listening to ourselves begins, a little lower, a little deeper, in the heart and gut of us. When we get still, reaching that still place inside, we discover whole worlds within us and, often, whole new levels of peace we didn't know before. We come back home to ourselves.

"Yoga changed so much," Taryn said. "The more I made it a regular practice, the more it changed the ways I looked at things." There it was, again, that new vision. She began welcoming in a gratitude practice to her days. "That doesn't mean I don't ever complain," she laughed as she explained it to me. But, now, she takes notice of what makes her heart happy. Of the little joys, the moments that make her and her whole family feel a little more whole, a little fuller, a little more connected. "I can look at a situation now and see something good in it, still."

Yoga also changed her relationship to her body. "Even the physical aspect of yoga—I just felt the best physically. I can exercise, I can do all those other things, but if I do them without doing yoga, I just don't physically feel like myself."

"Mmmhmm," I said, like saying an "amen" to her sermon on yoga. Preach it, girl. I felt the same way.

"And even with my third and fourth pregnancies," she went on, having such a regular yoga practice, my body was completely different. I always attribute that to yoga."

*

If you visit the Iris Mind + Body website, which is the home of Taryn's yoga studio that she co-owns with her partner Kristin, you'll find what I'm calling a declaration on their landing page. In the age of *yoga as exercise* and more performative yoga, especially as Instagram enters the yoga space, what she and Kristin are declaring is a little bit bold. They write:

"We aren't changing Yoga. Yoga for us remains rooted in the deep history and spirituality of the practice. We are just shattering the notion that Yoga has to be done a certain way, by certain bodies, at certain ages…If you have a body and an open mind, you have a Yoga body."

Yes, yoga is for everyone. The size and shape of your body does not determine whether you deserve to step onto a yoga mat and savor your own unique practice. In other words, Taryn and Kristin are inviting you in —their studio is a space that is open to all, that will welcome you without judgment or expectations. This is about love, not perfection.

This is the same way I hope I teach yoga—as a space that invites and celebrates all. So I smiled when I read about Taryn's mission and I told her this when we spoke. "I love your mission of connecting to all bodies," I told her. "Because yoga is for anyone. It's an experience that connects you to your heart."

"Exactly!" she said. "And what breaks my heart is I feel like people are afraid to go and try yoga because of this image that they have in their head. Or they say, *I can't touch my toes.* And I say, *Great, me either. I couldn't touch my toes, either! Just try.* And I guess because of how much yoga has changed me, I feel bad when people are selling themselves short. That's what we're trying to change at our studio."

This mission to make all people feel safe and welcomed in yoga, like they belong, matters. And this mission extends not only to people of different sizes and shapes and levels of flexibility, but to people of all ways of being. Taryn's older daughters take kids' yoga classes. But it's not just them. She and Rhea, at just 3 ½ months old, have already started a Baby and Me yoga class. "I've read about how yoga helps people with Down syndrome, with muscle tone and flexibility," she said, "so I definitely plan on pushing it on her…not that I want to push anything on anyone," she added after a moment. We both laughed. "But, I mean, yoga's not a bad thing to push on people, right?"

"Absolutely."

*

But the people Taryn wants to reach most are the moms.

Even before Rhea was born, Taryn explained, "I always said moms are my favorite clients because I feel they're the ones I can relate to the most and they're the ones who need it the most."

But this new journey with Rhea has clarified her mission. During her pregnancy with Rhea, which after the diagnosis became filled with extra appointments and lots of new information and expectations thrown at her, she said yoga helped ground her. "Because you can get your head in the clouds from time to time with all the things you feel you have to think about with this type of stressful pregnancy…yoga was that solace for me, bringing everything back to reality," she said. "It reminded me: This is just a baby. You're just pregnant. Don't worry about all the extra stuff."

And, so, I wanted to know the ways welcoming Rhea into her life changed her, not just as a mom, but as a teacher. Because I'm certain that when my life shifts, the way I teach shifts or the way I see yoga or my students shifts. We are always shifting and blooming in new ways, discovering new ways of expressing ourselves and expressing our bodies in yoga class.

I think this is what makes yoga so compelling. When you join together to take a class, the experience is both personal and collective. We practice as we are, honoring our bodies as they are, trying not to let what anyone else's practice looks like determine what ours should look like. And, yet, we feel the energy of the room, the beautiful wave of collective hearts and bodies in motion, including the energy of the teacher who's guiding us, creating space for us.

As teachers, we bring our personal changes to our classes. So while we all share the same catalog of poses—downward dog, dancer's pose, Warrior II— every teacher is different because we all call on these poses in our own ways; we bring to the class who we are; it is unavoidable. And it shouldn't be avoided. We are called to be teachers to bring a message only we can bring. Don't hide what makes you unique; embrace it. Shower the world with your unique fragrance.

This means Taryn's message as a teacher has shifted since giving birth to Rhea. She still believes in her mission to make yoga welcoming to all and in its power to offer peace in moments of stress and overwhelm. But she's refined it, deepened it.

"You know, I'm new," she said. "I've been a special needs mom for 3 ½ months. I don't consider myself an expert. But what I can already feel is you have moms who are busy and you have special needs moms who have a whole extra level of things they're worried about, who have extra appointments—and I think that mom probably feels ten times more guilty taking time for herself than a typical mom. And I know how hard it was for me as a typical mom."

She went on, "I feel fortunate that I went through all of that, and realized that when you don't take care of yourself, it's ten times worse for your family, for you, for everybody. And I know that now. Regardless of what we've had going on with Rhea, I've kept up with what I need to keep up with to keep myself healthy. And I think, if I could share that with other special needs moms, that would be an important mission of mine. *Please, please, make time for yourself.* Because I can already feel that stress and how much harder it is, and I can already feel that so many of the moms I've met just pour their whole selves into their children— which is what you're supposed to do. But you have to leave that little extra space for yourself because you're better for your children, you're better for your partner, you're better for your whole family when you're taking care of yourself."

"I think that's a special thing," I said to her. "That your daughters will get to grow up and see a woman and a mom who's making lots of time and space for them, but who's also making time and space for herself. That changes everything. You matter, too."

*

At the end of our conversation, I asked Taryn two more questions. The first was, "If you had just a few words to describe Rhea, what would they be?"

Without missing a beat, Taryn said, "Spectacular."

Mmm, yes.

At two months old, Rhea had heart surgery. Taryn said, "Watching her go through open heart surgery was just—I was just like, *I'm in complete awe of her*. She was my hero. I've never gone through anything like that and I've never watched something like that. So the fact that it was my two month old—spectacular."

"I also describe her as sunshine," she went on. "Because getting the diagnosis felt like a little bit of a storm and it was such a stressful pregnancy that when she came, I just felt like, *Okay*"—and here she let out a sigh of relief—"here is this rainbow, this sunshine after all of that."

Yes, a ray of sunshine. Breathe deep, mama. Your girl is magical.

*

every cloud

a prayer

every rain

drop

a miracle

—Francisco X. Alarcón

*

As much as this book is a celebration of individuals with Down syndrome, it has never been just about them. This is about community—all of us together. About love. About truth—human stories, human lives, Down syndrome or not. Each person I spoke to felt like a messenger, telling their own journey, dropping little blessings on me and us as they went— little reminders or lessons waiting for whoever needs them to pick them up and carry on, this time a little lighter, with a subtle reminder of support: *You're not alone.*

And, so, before I ended the interview, I had one more question for Taryn. "This last piece," I said to her, "is because I want to pick up on what you said about centering you, centering moms, making sure you have space for you." I was trying to tell her that her space in this matters, of course. That I don't want to just see Rhea, I want to see her as the strong and resilient woman she is. I want to see Taryn.

"I know, for me, I'd probably get shy around answering this question, but I don't want you to be shy," I told her. I wanted her to not hide her light, to not dim herself or lessen herself. I wanted her to stand in her own light and truth, exactly as she is.

"Okay," she said. "Yeah."

"So if you could choose a few words to describe yourself, to celebrate yourself—who you are—what would you say?"

She paused for a moment. "Umm," she said. But a moment later, she knew: "Determined," she said. "For sure, determined."

"I don't like to let," she paused again, deciding to reframe her answer, this time with embers of passion behind her words. "I opened up a yoga studio while I had three kids already and a job because it's kind of like the dreams don't have limits thing."

Earlier, Taryn had explained to me that her dreams for Rhea are not specific goals. Instead, she dreams that Rhea will "never have to say Down syndrome is stopping her from doing anything...I just want her to have opportunities and not to say *I can't because I have Down syndrome.* I want her to be able to set a goal for herself and work towards it."

"I imagine that's similar—minus the Down syndrome part," I said, "to your goals for your other daughters. That they can do whatever they set their hearts and minds on."

"Exactly, exactly," she said. "Dreams don't have limits."

So when Taryn opened a yoga studio with three children and a job, she was showing them, in her own way, that dreams don't have limits. "I just feel like there's no reason to put your dreams on hold," she added. "Things might not go as quickly as you want them to when you have other things going on, but we all have one life to live. So do what you need to do to be as happy as possible.

"So, yes, I am determined. Determined. Strong. And grateful."

These are the seeds that empower her and that grow empowered daughters. Because she is raising her daughters—all of them—to dream big.

Even if the world tells you *no*, follow your heart.

Because, if you believe it from deep within you, then *yes, yes, you can*.

*

Keep some room in your heart
for the unimaginable.

—Mary Oliver

*

The Peacemaking Mama

Kayla Craig is the mom of four children, including one daughter with Down syndrome, Eliza, whom she and her husband adopted and welcomed into their forever family.

"I definitely grew up playing with dolls and imagining —I've always had a very active imagination, and I was always creating. Every doll I had had to have a unique name...I've always had this creative spirit and kind of a mothering spirit, like always I hoped one day, maybe, I would get to be a parent. But I don't think I ever could have, in my wildest dreams, thought of what my family looks like today."

—Kayla Craig

When Kayla describes her family today, she calls it "unexpected," something she and her husband prayed for without really knowing they were praying for it. "We had open hands," she said, like they were ready to receive whatever life placed in them. "How we all came together as a family," she told me, "is really special, like a knitting together...of these different threads."

*

Today, Kayla, her pastor-husband Jonny, and their four children live in Midwest Iowa in Des Moines. "There are lots of corn fields," Kayla laughed. Kayla is a journalist and a producer for the *Love Anyway* podcast, a podcast that's part of Preemptive Love, a peacemaking organization that does the real work of choosing and cultivating love over violence. She's also a co-host of her own podcast about justice, faith, and culture. And at the center of it all, she is a mama who is intentional about raising her family and growing with them.

Twelve years ago, Kayla and Jonny got married. "We were newly married, in our early twenties," she told me, not really thinking about starting a family yet. When she was a little girl naming all her dolls, she hoped that motherhood would be part of her future, but she never imagined adoption. But, newly married, she kept having these dreams she "couldn't shake," dreams about adoption.

"It felt so out of the blue," she told me.

"Do you think it was a sign?" I asked her about these unexpected messages that came to her at night.

"Yes," she said. Because it was so unexpected, she told me she felt like she was paying more attention to it, like it had caught her awareness. These dreams morphed into more, "little things" here and there, she said, small signs that could have been easy to miss had they not been so surprising. They were little signs she would catch on the radio or on TV. "It felt like this continual messaging." But she wasn't quite sure how to bring this up to her husband: what do you say, *My dreams keep telling me we're supposed to adopt?*

But one day she and her husband were in the car, driving to visit their parents. "He turned off the radio," Kayla told me, "and he was like, 'Okay, I need to talk to you about something.' And I was like, 'I know what you're gonna say!' And he was like, 'I think, when we have kids, we should consider adoption.' And I said, 'Oh my gosh, I was thinking the same thing, too.'"

"It felt like affirmation," she said, "because I honestly didn't know how to bring it up." But there it was, again, the messages not only weaving their way into her dreamworld but into Jonny's mind, too.

Eventually, Kayla and Jonny welcomed Joseph into their family, a little boy who was living in an orphanage in Nigeria that couldn't find a family locally to place him with. "We prayed about it," Kayla told me, and they knew this is how they wanted to build their family. "It was not easy," but it was their way.

*

After Joseph came Asher, their biological son, and a few years later Kayla was pregnant with Abram. But before Abram came to be, Kayla and Jonny felt a calling, "a sensing," she called it, that they would be open to adopting a child with special needs. "We just did a home study," she told me, meaning they were laying the groundwork without actively pushing forward with another adoption. Again, their hands were open, "just ready," she said. But nothing materialized.

Nothing materialized, that is, until four months into her pregnancy with Abram. Four months into her pregnancy with Abram, Kayla got an email: there was a little girl, two and a half weeks old, still in the hospital, who happened to have Down syndrome and needed an adoptive family—did Kayla and Jonny want to welcome her into their own?

Kayla was at her computer when she read the email; she remembers balancing the computer on her belly as she read it. "I had two young kids, one more on the way, and all the logic would say, *What are you doing?*" Kayla said. "And yet I felt like this was such a gift and an honor, a privilege." Trusting her intuition and doing a little research by watching YouTube videos of adults with Down syndrome, she and her husband flew to Florida, where Eliza, their little girl with Down syndrome, was in the hospital.

"What were you feeling as you were flying down to Florida?" I asked her.

"I felt all the feelings," she laughed. "It happened so fast. It was Christmastime and I was really emotional to have to leave my kids, not ever normally leaving them on Christmas...I was nervous, afraid, anxious, wondering if I could be enough for her." But when Kayla held Eliza for the first time, all her initial fears melted away. "She was so tiny," Kayla said. "She was three weeks old and she was smaller than what my biological son was when he was born. She was just so petite and beautiful." That's when she knew: this unexpected family, and this unexpected addition of Eliza to her world, was meant to be. In that moment, Kayla told me she realized she had "prayed for Eliza without even knowing who she was." Holding her, she felt like all the threads were coming together.

"I mean, it's not like I held her and then everything was rainbows and butterflies," she clarified, not wanting to give a magical illusion of the realities of adoption and parenting. "Parenting in general is hard, and special needs parenting has a whole other set of things, but I think, when I held her, all those initial anxieties and worries went away and I realized, *This is just a baby. We don't have to have everything figured out now.*"

Kayla, Jonny, and Eliza arrived back home in Iowa by New Years and, a few months later, Abram was born.

She had four young children in her home at once, two under 6 months old. "It could have been really hard, but it was such a beautiful time together," she said. Sure, there were tears and lots of coffee and naps and the grace and support of her community. But Kayla cherished it. Describing having two infants at once, she said, "They were both such a gift."

*

Kayla's family looks a little different. Joseph and Eliza have their own shades of dark skin, while Asher and Abram do not. And, so, sometimes other children are curious and ask questions. Kayla told me that kids may ask, "How can they be siblings: they do not look alike." And even adults may ask, "Are those your *real* kids?"

"Someone might not mean it maliciously," Kayla says, but those questions hurt because "there's an extra layer of pain and grief when someone outside eludes, 'Well, that's not your *real* mom.'"

Kayla told me, of course, she's their mom—"I was the one getting up in the middle of the night and changing a diaper and feeding them. In our family, the kids are the kids and the mom and dad are the mom and dad. And adoption is forever in our family. That is what we've committed to." So rather than getting angry at other adults who ask these questions, Kayla uses it as a teaching opportunity. Anger doesn't heal, but love and understanding does. And, usually, they get it. "Most people are like, 'Oh, yeah, yeah. Totally,'" she said.

There's also an invisible trauma in adoption, Kayla told me, "the trauma of losing their biological family." I once heard another mom of an adoptive daughter describe it as a "primal wound." And, so, it's important for Kayla and her family to talk about and affirm what makes a family a family. Are they her *real* kids? Of course they are. "It's just that all families look different," she tells her kids. "And this is just what our family looks like. And we are so real!" she said, laughing. "We're not fake. We're not pretend. I feel like words matter," meaning the way we talk about our own families and other families is not something to take lightly; we must speak about ourselves and others with love and intention and kindness. Curiosity is okay, too, but as long as we lean into our curiosity with a compassionate heart.

"So give me a glimpse into one of these conversations," I said to Kayla. "If you were with your kids right now, how might you talk to them about what a family is."

Kayla told me they've had different conversations based on different ages. But "if I were talking to them on the couch right now, I'd be like, 'What does a family do? A family is a team. We are always on each other's side.' We talk about the boys that are brothers, that are rambunctious, and how we are not harming each other but we're helping each other heal and have hope and encourage each other. Another thing we say is, 'Families stick together like glue. We are close, and we are cheering each other on, and when we make mistakes, we apologize and forgive and we repair the harm that has been done.'" She went on, "And then there are very tangible things like, 'Families clean up together.' And, 'Families read a story before bed. Families take a walk in the neighborhood. Families can do lots of different things, but we all end up home together.'" And then she laughed, "And with the pandemic, we've all been home together 24/7 for months now." Some things in life are unexpected.

"It's so heartening for me to hear the way you're raising your children," I told her, "with peace and awareness and all that good stuff."

"We try," she laughed. Later, she would use the word "intentional" to describe her mothering. "Ah, yes," I said, getting it. "You raise them with intention."

*

When Eliza was a baby, she was diagnosed with infantile spasms. It's a type of epilepsy, and "it was pretty devastating for her," Kayla said. For a while, they struggled to find a medication that could help her, which meant the spasms kept happening. "She got so swollen from the wrong medications. I look back at those pictures and it breaks my heart for her…because there was a point where she didn't smile."

For a while, Kayla wondered whether she was ever going to get to see her daughter again for who she is, a child who smiles, who can feel safe and well enough to be present in the moment, to be all of her. With much grace, the spasms are under control now. But since then, Kayla and Jonny have gone on many medical journeys with her.

In a recent Instagram post, Kayla described a little of what life with Eliza, who is now four years old, may look like each day. "Life right now, for us, looks like this: Measuring g-tube formula and meds on little sleep. Three meals by mouth, spoonful by spoonful every day. Diaper changes every few hours knowing diapers might always be our reality. AFOs [ankle foot orthotics] and abdominal binders and knee immobilizers. Language therapy, speech therapy, occupational therapy. Emails after emails with surveys about her disabilities from the school district disability team as they plan for four-year-old preschool…"

Sometimes, motherhood is challenging and tiring.

For years, Kayla, in her minivan, would drive past a fence in her neighborhood that was painted with the phrase, "Bloom where you are planted." She didn't always love the phrase. "I hated it," she said, laughing. She thought that "it felt cliché at best and oppressive at worst." She felt like it was whispering, "Stay where someone puts you, be quiet, don't complain, look pretty."

But, in recent months, she has come to see the phrase in a new light. Perhaps it can also mean: Can I flourish where I am, exactly where my roots are planted in this moment?

"I want to talk to you about that phrase," I told her, but this time I wanted to know what it was like to bloom in the midst of challenging medical journeys, when you're worried for your child, when you're searching for the best path ahead, when you're trying to create the best present and future for them. I liked that Kayla spoke honestly about her daily life with Eliza and I wanted her to share that with others who may be struggling, too, who may think they're alone or not living up to what their child with different abilities or a medical journey needs. "What nourishing words might you offer to other parents of children going their own own medical journey?" I asked her. "Because maybe they need a gentle and loving

69

reminder that parenting can be challenging and exhausting and, still, they are enough. In other words, how do you bloom in sometimes rocky soil?"

"That's so good," Kayla said, "because I need those words, too. I think we always—parents or not parents —wonder if we're the only ones who feel the way we feel and it's really easy, especially with special needs parenting—it's kind of physically isolating if you're pushing a wheelchair or you're running from therapy to therapy. Your life might not look quite like your other friends' lives. So I think we can get in our heads and tell ourselves stories of, *Well, I'm the only one who feels the way I do.* And you kind of feel even more isolated. So just knowing you're not alone, no one is perfect, everyone has those moments of fear about the future, of exhaustion, of just being tired is important. And it's kind of a cliché, but you can't pour from an empty cup. So knowing the things in your life you can incorporate to take care of yourself is helpful. Having someone in your life you can speak to honestly. Finding other parents, even if it's just digitally, that are taking similar journeys with their kids. Those are all things that help those feelings of isolation and exhaustion."

Because while Kayla's day-to-day life with Eliza may include many extra forms of care that other parents don't go through—and this is real and can be challenging—what Kayla also told me about her life with Eliza is that it is "unfettered joy." It is "brimming," she said, overflowing with love.

"Eliza has so many needs," Kayla said. "She is so dependent. She also is so—she just radiates so much love."

Eliza doesn't walk or use her hands much or speak verbally, but she communicates joy and love and everything she's feeling—the whole range we have as human beings—in her own very meaningful ways.

Kayla and I are both writers. "I think one of the things I've learned as a writer," I said to her, "is that speech is a form of power in this world. As a writer, being able to articulate what other people may be feeling but perhaps struggle to put into words themselves, it is valued. But I also believe we—all of us—communicate in silence, in energy, in a love that extends from our hearts. And, to me, this is another form of inner power. So tell me some of the ways Eliza communicates with you and her world."

"Yes," Kayla said, "just because she's not verbal doesn't mean she's not communicating." Kayla described the way Eliza touches her face "and looks right into me," she said, "and I feel so seen and loved. She might never be able to sign, 'I love you,' but she can tell me 'I love you' with her hand on my cheek and that feels like such a gift. And to see her laugh feels like such a gift because we remember when she was on so much medicine that she couldn't even laugh. So we don't know what the future is and there will be more challenges along the way. But we're not called to worry about the future. We're just in the present right now, and Eliza helps me pay attention to the present and she helps me find joy in the everyday.

"And it's not like Eliza doesn't have days where she doesn't want to participate in therapy or she doesn't want to play or she's grouchy—we're all human and we all have a broad range of emotion, but there is something that's just so special about Eliza that I can barely put into words that really makes the worries and anxieties and the sheer amount of work it takes sometimes to help her get what she wants—it really puts it in perspective."

Eliza has the innate power to make her mother and her family feel seen. And Kayla told me it's not just with them, "she just radiates it to others, too." This is rare and precious, because isn't that what we're all searching for? To be seen as we are? To be known and loved as we are?

Eliza is not perfect. "We don't want her to be some inspirational prop," Kayla told me. She is human and on her own human journey full of peaks and valleys and everything in between. But with her sweet soul, she lightens the load of those around. She is a seer, seeing from her soul into ours, and that is a gift.

A few months ago, Kayla described on Instagram the "unfettered joy" that is Eliza. "I see Asher," Kayla wrote of Eliza's older brother, "gently sit with Eliza, letting her pull his hair and touch his face for hours as he watches a movie with her, and he tells me, 'She might never talk, but I know what she is telling me.'"

And there our hearts go, broken wide open.

*

Hello, sun in my face.
Hello you who made the
morning and spread it over the
fields…Watch, now, how I
start the day in happiness,
in kindness.

—Mary Oliver

*

Kayla is a producer for the *Love Anyway* podcast. It's a show created to move its listeners "beyond fear, beyond the simple narrative of *us vs. them*." Its message is inclusion—when we look to the other people of the world and even people nearby who we think are so unlike us, perhaps when we truly come to see them, to connect with them, to listen to them, we will realize they are not so unlike us after all. That we can actively choose to honor each other, that we can actively choose love and peace.

Because the form of love that shows up as peace in the world is not simply something that happens, that we can just wait for. We have been taught to fear what's different or what's uncertain—what we don't know—and this too often has pushed us to reject rather than embrace all beings, no matter who they are or how they're born or where they come from. But Kayla believes peace is something that we must choose over and over again. You can passively try to keep peace or you can actively make peace. Kayla is a peace*maker.*

Her children are still young (Joseph is the oldest at ten years old), but I wanted to know how she teaches her children the work of peace. "You're raising children who may live different experiences than you did growing up, not just because they're different people, of course, living in a different time in our world but because, on a simple level, two of them don't look like you. How do you equip yourself for that—how do you help prepare them and prepare yourself for the world they will greet?" I asked her. What I was trying to know was, how is she showing up in the conversation around race and racial justice—and does it matter?

"It matters deeply," she answered. "I can't imagine the disservice I would be doing my kids if I did not care about racial equity and racial justice...Not just diversity," she added, "but really creating a more beautiful world for them where they are honored and not hurt or harmed just because of the color of their skin."

A few months ago, Kayla wrote what she called a "deeply personal prayer," a "prayer for her black son." "I am a white woman raising a black son," she wrote, and a black daughter, too. Her prayer begins,

He loves LEGOs, O Lord
And superheroes, and riding his bike
But I am afraid to let him ride alone
Because our world is not safe for boys who look like him

...Will he see his belovedness, O Lord?
When he looks in the mirror
In his black skin and tight curls?

...Help me work to make a better world

THE PEACEMAKING MAMA

For my son, my beloved son…

Kayla's mothering includes fear and worry, but also asking the real questions about how we make the world better for children that look like hers, like Joseph and Eliza, and for all children, including Asher and Abram. How does she raise intentional, compassionate, and safe children, wishing that all four of them, regardless of their color, will be safe and will be able to shine their unique light?

So she talks to them about peace. "We talk to them about how we want all kids to have a family and be with their families." This is the work of peace. "So if they hear something at school or on the news, then we actively enter into that conversation and, hopefully, in an age-appropriate way but in a way that says, for us, we're people of faith and we believe God desires everyone to be cared for and to be safe. So we talk about that."

Kayla's children are also often hearing her talk about the work Preemptive Love, a global peacemaking organization where she is a podcast producer, does. "They're hearing me talk about the work we're doing in Iraq and Syria and Mexico and Venezuela to empower people whose lives have been devastated by war and violence. So we talk about that, too. And then, on a smaller scale," and here she laughs, "we talk about, *If you harm your brother, then we need to talk about it and see what those consequences are and trying to repair it."*

I thought that was so powerful, the way she points her children not only to the consequences of their actions if they, say, push their brother, but repairing it. We grow not just by feeling the guilt of our sins, but atoning for them—actively learning and listening to the other person tell us how our actions hurt them and then working to make it better or working to help heal as best we can. This is where true peace comes from. Our society is too often built around systems of punishment, but true change will come when we don't center external punishment, but inner growth and understanding. This is love.

"In my generation, in watching the world" Kayla said, "I sometimes heard things said and not done. I want our kids to be awake and paying attention and to lead with compassion and empathy. And to know that sometimes, speaking up, someone will say, *you shouldn't do that*, but if you know it's the right thing to do, to have the courage and bravery to do it."

Later, when I would put her on the spot and ask her to tell me what peace or peacemaking is, she said, "That's a hard one because sometimes it depends on what context…probably something along the lines of being open-hearted, being willing to do justice and love mercy and walk humbly with your God…But I

would have to give it more thought," she said
modestly.

Even without time to give it more thought, her vision
of peace moved me.

*

I wish I knew how
It would feel to be free
I wish I could break
All the chains holding me

—Nina Simone

*

At the end of our conversation, I laughed and told Kayla, "We're going to play a game now...of finish the sentence." She was kind enough to agree and go along with it. So a few times in a row, I'd read her the beginning of a sentence, a new one each time, and I'd ask her to finish it.

"Love is…" I said.

"The final fight," she said, quoting John Perkins, a man born in 1930 in the deep South who was faced with violent racism. Instead of bitterness, he discovered within him that final fight, the fight to love and forgive, instead.

"God is…" I said.

"Always pursuing us."

"Mmm, yes," I said, a reminder that we are never lost.

"My family is…"

"A gift," she said.

"I am…" I started.

"Grateful," she said. I could tell, she was. Every day, she lives her life choosing gratitude. Just like peace, this is not something that just happens, that just comes. We need to choose it, over and over again.

Lastly, I asked her, "Eliza is…"

"Oh, my goodness!" she lit up. "This is a hard one because she's so many things." But she came back to that one line that seems to celebrate and define Eliza the most to Kayla. "Unfettered joy," she said.

Yes, unfettered joy.

*

Despite all the challenges Kayla has faced as a mother and a peacemaker—as a human—she seems to confront her fears with grace. "What gives you solace in moments of fear?" I asked her, referring specifically to her journey with Eliza when she's not sure what's ahead.

"I have been praying," she told me. "But not in the way I thought prayer needed to be or should be. I have been writing out my prayers and doing breath prayers and I feel like that is very centering. It roots me down and helps me be focused."

"A breath prayer—is that something you do as a practice," I asked her, "like you sit down and think, 'Inhale' and here you inhale into your prayer, and 'Exhale,' and here you exhale your prayer to the world?"

"Yes, yes," she said. "And sometimes I just incorporate it into my day. I can do it while I'm taking care of kids or making food or running errands or doing whatever little things I'm doing."

"I like that," I said. "When I'm not writing, I'm a yoga teacher and, in yoga, we do intentional breath work. We set intentions or personal prayers for our practice, what we want to cultivate on and off our yoga mats. But I think, sometimes, we think we have to set out this whole hour for a yoga class in order to be intentional, to say our personal prayers, to do our deep breathing. But the better question is how do we take all of that and bring it into the rest of our lives? Bringing intention into your life doesn't have to be one big event, that we have to rework our lives around it to make room for it. It can be in the simple things, the everyday things, the small moments. It can be carried through at any time. In the midst of our lives, we can still bring intention into our breath."

As I finished talking, Kayla's dog Olive jumped on her lap. Kayla had been sitting outside in her yard, on a porch swing, and Olive came running through the door and onto her mama's lap.

"Besides Olive," I teased, "and besides breath prayer, what are the things that nourish you, that light you up, that you do to take care of you so you can have a full —an overflowing—cup?" Again, I wanted to know what helped her bloom. Because we cannot nourish others if we are not first nourishing our own roots.

"I love writing," she told me. "I love reading." And here we dished on our favorite books and I vowed to pick up a copy of *Walking on Water* from my local library because it's one of Kayla's favorites. But what also lights up Kayla is the people she loves—that sense of community, of connection, of cherishing and nourishing each other. "I love being outside and just going on a walk with my family," she said. "It's such a good reset, with the fresh air and sunshine. And just laughter—pursuing laughter and joy because life is so heavy. My husband is so funny and I think, sometimes, I'm funny, too, and just spending time together and making each other laugh."

Kayla has been married for twelve years now, and they're still laughing. I smiled.

"Okay, this is the last question, I promise," I told her. I wanted to know what I didn't know—what hadn't I asked that she thought was an important part of telling her story. In her true and intentional fashion, Kayla considered what others might need to hear from her journey.

"I'm not a superhero," she said. "My husband and I are not superheroes for adopting. We're just human. We're just normal people that mess up all the time and have to say sorry all the time, but it's really a gift to parent Eliza. And I say that also knowing that she's a beautiful child in body and soul and sometimes she's naughty and she gets in trouble." In other words, she's not perfect and, as Kayla told me earlier, it's not all rainbows and butterflies. That's not human. That's not real. "But there is a lot that she has shown us just by being exactly who she is. And it's helped me be more gentle with myself. Because I think, the way she sees me, and that light and love in her eyes—the way God looks at all of us—it helps us see that this life is not about how much we can do or achieve. And when we do things, that's great. But, ultimately, our value and belovedness isn't in that.

"If you ever have anyone in your life who helps you do that, that's wonderful," Kayla said. "And, for me, that person has been Eliza."

Without needing to change a thing about her, Eliza has showered Kayla and her world with so much beauty.

This is love.

*

While love could swallow one whole as the ocean does rain, we somehow manage to carry it in our hearts and on our sleeves. It is of us, and bigger than all of us.

—Mikey Berryman

*

I wanted you more than ever you will know, so I sent love to follow you wherever you go.

—Nancy Tillman

*

The Beauty

Grace Strobel is a model and an advocate based in Missouri.
She happens to have Down syndrome.
Linda Strobel is her mom.

The first time I spoke to Grace and her mom, Linda, together, I was taken aback by their beauty. "Wow, you can see the mother-daughter resemblance," I told them, referring to their long, flowing blonde hair and natural beauty. They both smiled in an "aw, shucks" kind of way.

When I began to consider writing this book, I knew I wanted to include a model with Down syndrome. I wanted to explore beauty in all its facets. But as I told Grace and her mom later, I didn't choose to speak with them, specifically, just because Grace is beautiful on the outside (she is, of course, just as we all are—each blooming in our own ways). I chose Grace because she expresses a deeper beauty. She's a model with a mission.

I'm the founder of an organic skincare line and, so, the question of beauty has been on my mind for years. In fact, for a while, I struggled to find my way within my skincare line because I was certain I didn't want to be part of the *beauty industry*, that I wanted to celebrate each person's beauty exactly as it is and not offer them products that make them feel that anything about the way they look needs to be fixed—wrinkles, lines, marks; embrace it all. I've come to say that the mission of my line, beyond honoring your skin and working in tune with our planet, is to connect you to the beauty of your soul. So speaking to Grace, a model who has had to overcome all these barriers to show the world her innate beauty, who has had to shout her worth over and over again—it felt a little personal to me. Because Grace's beauty is real and true, but it is her soul beauty that is the most stunning thing about her.

When I would later ask her, *What makes someone beautiful?,* she would tell me:

"I think it's what's inside someone. I think it's kindness in someone's heart that makes them beautiful." And she would add, "And it's how they treat others." Compassion is beauty, too.

This, a beauty of the heart, is the kind of beauty we all need to rally around. And Grace is the kind of leader who can help show us the way.

*

I met Grace first through photos. Like so many influencers these days, she's leveraging the power of social media to spread her message, and so I first saw her smile through her Instagram posts. And it's quite a smile, filling any space she's in, popping off the page of her photos. When I would eventually ask her to describe herself, she told me she's smart (she is), she's funny, she's a hard worker, and she's joyful. It's true—she has this natural (no pun intended) grace about her, this natural love that makes me feel love and joy in her presence; it's like sunshine. She's got that "it" factor about her, something almost unnameable but undoubtedly felt. Wordlessly, she connects to us.

After scrolling through her photos, I started listening to her speak, watching old interviews she gave. And, immediately, I could see how intelligent she is. Her mom would later tell me, "She has so much up here," and she pointed to her head. But what comes through even more than her poise when she speaks and her intelligence is what's in her heart.

"There's so much in your heart that you share with the world," I told her, "whether it's through your words or your energy. That felt so apparent to me the first time I saw your photos. Who you are comes through."

"Thank you," she said, smiling.

Perhaps this is what makes Grace so naturally fitted to model. Being in front of a camera can feel vulnerable. For me, I often shrink before a camera lens, afraid to take up too much space, to be seen in too much light, to let who I am out. But Grace doesn't hide. She's doesn't hide her beauty or her light. She opens herself up and invites the lens of the camera and everyone who will view her photos in. It's as if she is so at home within herself, so accepting of who she is, that she feels safe to share her joy and her essence with the world.

This is why she is a natural.

As natural as she is, though, getting to this point both personally and collectively was not easy. Grace is changing the face of beauty, and that is revolutionary. She has had to work to show the world that she belongs here as a model. That she deserves to take up space, to be seen, and to shine her full light.

*

Yes, Grace is a pioneer, paving the way. Go back a decade, or even five years, and I'm not sure we could name so many prominent models with Down syndrome—or any. The industry wasn't representing *all* shades of beauty.

And representation matters.

So many of our dreams become real when we have what I like to call "spirit-helpers," people showing us and telling us that our dreams are possible. That *we can*. And part of knowing we can, part of truly internalizing it, is seeing that there is a path for us, seeing others like us leading the way. Seeing that, if we have Down syndrome, we, too, can model. Or we, too, can follow our own dreams, whatever they may be. It's nourishing and buoying to see people like us doing what we've always longed to do, being reminders that our way is possible. Grace is this reminder.

When Barack Obama became the first black president, whether you celebrate his politics or not, he let young black children know that the presidency is possible for them, too: he expanded the White House's reach, allowing more children to touch it, to claim it as their own. Because now it wasn't some fantasy: they could see it with their own eyes—*a man who looks like me is president*. This is why one of my favorite photos of him during his presidency is not him posing with some great leaders of other nations, but him standing with his head leaning towards the floor in the middle of the Oval Office, allowing a little boy of color to touch his hair and see: *oh, it's just like mine.*

I can be president, too.

*

Just like Barack Obama, Grace is a spirit-helper and a forerunner. "I want to keep modeling and speaking," she told me, "to help people rethink what is possible…we all have gifts and talents, and I want to use mine to help others."

What Grace is doing, simply by being who she is and letting the world see her light, is she's letting all people, especially children with Down syndrome, know that they have value, too, no matter who they are or how many chromosomes they're born with. She's letting young people with Down syndrome know that they deserve to be seen and heard, and isn't that what we're all looking for? Isn't that one of the most powerful means of uplifting someone, by letting them know: *I see you, you matter. Your dreams are possible, too.*

But unlike the children she's inspiring, Grace's case is a little unusual since she stepped into modeling without many examples preceding her. In fact, perhaps it has always felt like a calling to her, as if something has been whispering to her, pointing her on her way. Long before there was any space for people with Down syndrome in the modeling world, Grace was asking her mom if she could model. When I asked her if she ever expected to grow up and be a model when she was a little girl, without missing a beat, she responded, "Oh, yeah!" She always knew this was in her and that she could do it—"I am capable," she told me, "and I can do the same things as everyone else."

If fact, Grace told me that modeling, even the first time she ever did a professional photoshoot, doesn't make her nervous. "Oh, no," she said. "I wasn't nervous. It was fun." The hardest part, she explained, of any photoshoot is just when it's a long day and they're moving from location to location and, so, she doesn't have much time to eat. "I'm hungry then," she laughed.

(When she's not running around during a photoshoot, she likes to eat salads, although pizza is her favorite.)

Grace was born this way—born to model. And she has navigated her path with such determination and belief that it's as if she has always greeted life like there are no limits beyond the ones we place on ourselves.

*

The thing is, knowing something in your bones—
feeling your destiny in you—doesn't mean stepping
into it is easy.

These days, Grace is insistent that kindness matters.
"No matter who you are," she told me, "we want all
the same things: to be valued, to be respected, and to
feel good about ourselves."

When I asked why she believes so ardently in
kindness, so told me that, growing up, she was bullied.
"Our whole life—it's been challenging," Linda told
me. "I'm not going to say it's been a joyride. There
have been many hurtful times."

"Yes," Grace said, acknowledging what her mom said.
"I felt that same thing," she added, referring to
bullying. "And I wanted to change that for others."

Because Grace has known pain, she is now
overflowing with compassion. After persistent
bullying and talks with her parents, she finally said,
"Mom, I don't want anyone else to feel like this." She
wanted to use her experiences, all of her pain, and she
wanted to transform it, to let others know that
bullying is never okay.

So even before Grace began modeling, her parents
helped her build a presentation for school children.
Speaking to students, Grace would take the unfamiliar

—Down syndrome—and bring it closer. We tend to fear what we don't know and by being in that room with those children, speaking her own story, she was showing them that what seemed so different is nothing to fear—she's just like them. "If we could help people to understand and not be afraid," her mom told me, "then it's going to help everybody." Because we all bloom when we all can bloom. "I just think that we need to name the purple elephant in the room," her mom went on, "and talk about how that feels. We're blessed that Grace can articulate her feelings and tell people how bullying really feels. That she's a human being first."

When children hear Grace speak, she connects. Just as she does as a model, she welcomes them in and shows them her light.

No, different is not scary. Love can replace fear.

*

*A spark of kindness
made a light.
The light made an
opening in the darkness.*

—Joy Harjo

*

When Grace was born 24 years ago, her parents didn't know she had Down syndrome. "Well, I had an inkling," her mom told me. At 16 weeks into the pregnancy, tests confirmed unusual protein levels, which could indicate Down syndrome. "But I wasn't going to do anything to the pregnancy, to end it," Linda said, "So I was always wondering," but she and her husband decided not to proceed with any more tests. What would be, would be.

But the curious thing is that Linda had been drawn to the world of Down syndrome long before Grace came into her life. "When I was going through middle school—a long time ago," she laughed, "we had very segregated classes and it always used to bother me to see the kids in the special education room having to be isolated, having to eat alone. I would always befriend some of them because I just felt—it was just such an isolation."

By the time she was in high school, Linda, still curious, decided to volunteer at a camp for children with special needs. "And, for some odd reason," she told me, "I was so drawn to the kids with Down syndrome."

"Now, this was before the Internet," she laughed again. So she would run home from camp each day and say to her mom, "Mom, can I go to the library?" At the library, she would check out all these books on

Down syndrome, always wanting to learn more. "Little did I know what life had in store for me…"

"Do you believe your attraction to these kids with Down syndrome when you were younger was a sort of signal, a divine sign?" I asked her. "Like you were always meant to welcome Grace into your life?"

"I do, I honestly do," she said. "I think, if you are open to God's signs, they're all right there."

Linda went on to tell me about all these signs, these "hints" she called them, that she had while she was pregnant with Grace. And as much as she felt a child with Down syndrome calling to her, she still worried, "and I hoped it wasn't Down syndrome," she said honestly. From working at that camp as a teenager, she thought she knew what Down syndrome was and, "I will tell you," she said, "it scared me. Because I dealt with and helped these kids all summer long— and that's not something you envision for your child. I'm just being blunt. That's not what you envision."

The problem wasn't Down syndrome so much as it was the world Down syndrome existed in 24 years ago when Grace was born, and even before that, when Linda worked at that camp in high school. "24 years ago was a very different time than it is now," Linda told me. Grace now lives with her family in Missouri, but she was born in California. Linda expected The Golden State to be more progressive, more welcoming to individuals of all abilities. But she was surprised by how much pressure she felt to abort her child at the mere hint of Down syndrome. "My doctor, when I said I wasn't going to get an amnio [to confirm Down syndrome], was absolutely shocked," Linda said. "And she made some kind of comment later on when I was getting an ultrasound and I was a little nervous about the health of the baby—she said, 'What? You're worried about it? I told you, you should have had the amnio so you could have done something about it.'

"I wouldn't have done anything about it," Linda asserted. "But it was such a pressure not to value that life." When Linda shared the news with a microbiology teacher of hers (she was taking a class at the time), the teacher echoed the same sentiments: "So what are you going to do about it?"

"It's overwhelming how much Down syndrome was stigmatized."

So when Grace was born 24 years ago, she wasn't ushered into a world full of celebration and joy at her arrival. "When she was born," Linda told me, "there was a very negative feeling in the room. It was dark, it was hushed, all the doctors and nurses were whispering. It was kind of like there was absolutely no joy in the room. It was, *this is a crisis*. It was, *Oh, my gosh, I'm so sorry.* It was like death," she said. "It was like death."

But there was one nurse in the room—"we'll never forget her," Linda told me. "Her name was Holly and she was just the nicest thing. And she said, 'Oh, she's so beautiful.' She was the very first person who said anything. Everyone else, all the joy was sucked out. And then, about an hour later, a geneticist came in and kind of just laid out the facts. 'She'll be heavy,' she said. 'She'll live with you the rest of her life. She'll never read. She'll never write.' And, 'You can adopt her out,' she said. Even in 1996, they said, 'You can still institutionalize her.'"

Linda went on, "That kind of gets you, when that's the first reaction to your child. So, I tell you, as a mother, that kind of lit a fire under me. I'm the kind of person who, if you tell me no, I'm going to do it. I didn't know how it was going to go, just that we had to work hard."

*

And she did. She and Grace did every single day.

On Grace's website, it says, "When faced with trials and adversity, we learn to have courage and be strong." I wanted to know what Linda learned about her own courage and strength while raising Grace.

"I definitely think mothers of children with disabilities have to have extraordinary courage every day," she told me. "Because we all know our children have value and worth and potential, but the everyday world sometimes doesn't."

We talked about the ways social media is changing the game, the way new and expecting parents are now greeted by a whole community, near and far, with support and love. With affirmation and congratulations. But "when you go out in the public," away from social media, Linda told me, "it can be very different."

"I find it the hardest thing to have to keep proving Grace's worth every single day," she told me. "I think, when Grace was growing up, my biggest struggle was low expectations. It was always not, *Let's try this*. It was, *These kids can't do this*. It was always, *the population*," as if they're some analogous group, indistinguishable and all destined to never rise from the limits placed upon them by the world. "Nobody ever really held the bar high," Linda said.

But in her own ways, Linda began to educate the people around her. One day when Grace was a toddler in a high chair, she and her family were out at a restaurant eating brunch. There was another family there, at a neighboring table, with two young kids. And the kids kept staring at Grace. "Which I totally get," Linda said. "As a kid, when you see someone who looks a little different, everyone is fascinated. But that family made it so uncomfortable for us to be in there. The kids would not stop staring at her."

This is when Linda had to have courage. "Until you're a mom," she told me, "you just can't imagine—you get these mama bear instincts where you feel very protective. Whatever you hold dear—if someone is gawking at it, it's very hard to look away," to not be bothered by it. So Linda finally got up from the table, picked Grace out of her high chair, and carried her over to the other family's table. "I said to the kids, 'Hey, I see you're interested. I wanted to bring her closer to you so you can look at her. Her name is Grace.' I kind of hit it straight on," she told me.

But Linda was doing more than protecting Grace or hitting it straight on, she was educating. She was quietly teaching those kids how to speak and connect across difference—and to realize there isn't that much different after all. She was centering Grace's personhood, her humanity. And she was gently showing those parents how to help their kids understand and interact with people with Down syndrome in the future. Instead of gawking or being silent about it, perhaps you get a little closer and say hello.

*

You cannot swim for new horizons until you have courage to lose sight of the shore.

—William Faulkner

*

Of course, today, Linda knows something about people with Down syndrome she didn't know 24 years ago when she anxiously worried if her daughter had Down syndrome or not. "This life with Grace," she told me, "it's incredibly fulfilling and rewarding." And as Grace rises into the spotlight as a speaker, an advocate, and a model, Linda says, "A lot of times it's hard to believe that it's happened. I always envisioned her life as something different than what was first diagnosed for her, I always believed in her, but I didn't know what that was...There are so many days when the reality of how many perceptions she's changing and how many lives she's changing and how many people she's giving hope to hits me and it kind of overwhelms me sometimes because I know she's making a difference."

Today, when Grace walks down a runway, it energizes her; she loves it. "I always wanted to be on stage," she told me, "like my sister Lainie," who grew up dancing. Walking on a runway, "it makes me feel so pumped. When I'm on the runway, I feel excited."

"What's everyone doing when you're on the runway?" her mom asked her.

"Clapping for me," she said, and then she mimes people blowing kisses at her.

Twenty-four years ago, the room was hushed when Grace entered it. But now it erupts when she walks through it, spotlighted in the center. Walking down a runway, it is a celebration, people cheering and sending her love. What a different world she has grown into and created with her attitude, her perseverance, and her self-belief.

"I love changing minds and hearts," she told me. "I love showing respect and what is possible...I have a great life."

"And what has Grace taught you?" I asked Linda.

"Unconditional love," she told me. "She doesn't hold grudges...And she has taught me true lessons in forgiveness." When Grace was bullied for so many years, Linda told me that Grace taught her not to hold on to the anger or the blame. Grace would simply let it go, carrying on with who she is. It doesn't mean it didn't hurt, but Grace let love triumph over anger. Through Grace, Linda "finally figured out that if we forgive, if we pray specifically for the people that hurt us, the pain kind of just goes away. Grace has taught me a lot about that. She's helped us shed some scales from our eyes and shown us what's really important."

Grace is grateful for all her family has shared with her, too, all the love and support and nourishment. When I asked her who the most beautiful person she knows is, she said, "My sister, Lainie." And then she added, "I love being with my dad."

"What does he make you feel like?" Linda asked her.

"He's so proud of me," she said. "He loves giving me hugs and kisses."

Linda and I paused for a collective, *Awww!*

"And I love when I scare him!" Grace laughed. She likes to hide around the corner sometimes and, when her dad comes in the door, she jumps out in surprise.

"You know he loves you, right?" Linda asked. "And he's so proud of you? We're both proud of you."

"Yes! Yes!" Grace smiled.

*

Authenticity is a big word for me. I use it often, I believe in it, I center my work around it. My message is, *Be who you are.*

But what I've also learned is that being who you are sometimes means getting bullied. It means that, sometimes, other people still won't try to make room for you, won't believe that you deserve equal space, equal protections, equal love. Being who you are is not always easy.

Grace's mom will tell you that her life has been challenging, that they've both had to shout Grace's worth over and over again, every single day. Linda has had to watch her own daughter being made to feel less by other children because she didn't look the same.

But despite all the struggles and challenges, the one rising feeling I felt at the end of my conversation with Grace and Linda wasn't pain, wasn't *You've got to hide your light if you're different because being who you are can be too painful.* It was hope.

It's why Grace is working so hard to make change, to show, as she said, "that we all have gifts and talents."

Despite everything they have been through, times are changing.

Grace is part of that wave of change. Showing who she is to the world matters.

When Grace was born, they told her mom not to value her life. To give her away, she wasn't worthy of their love or their family. She didn't have worth. What wasn't possible one generation ago is now made real in Grace. "I like modeling because it makes me feel good about myself," she said. Being seen in magazines and on posters at the mall doesn't make Grace feel like she needs to hide, like she must be ashamed of herself. Not only can Grace be herself amongst her family—in small, private spaces—she can shout her worth to everyone passing by. She can let her light out. She is what generations of self-advocates have been dreaming of. What seemed impossible one generation ago is now very real.

It doesn't mean we don't have more progress to make. It doesn't mean that everyone with Down syndrome has equal access to the supports that have made Grace's dreams possible. But she is a sign: change is here. And more is coming.

In one lifetime, Grace has made a shift: she represents a step toward creating a world where you can have Down syndrome and still dream big. Where you can have Down syndrome and still be seen as beautiful and worthy, where, as her mom says, you can be "respected not pitied."

THE BEAUTY

Someday, children with Down syndrome will grow up never knowing anything different. This is the world we've been dreaming of.

A world whose heart is big enough and open enough to love us all, exactly as we are.

*

Every woman that finally figured out her worth has picked up her suitcases of pride and boarded a flight to freedom, which landed in the valley of change.

—Shannon Alder

*

"Grace, what are your dreams?" I asked her.

She told me how she wants to keep doing what she's doing—modeling, speaking, showing the world what's possible.

For too long, we've been fed the idea—over and over again—that beauty comes only in one form. That it looks a certain way. But Grace is showing that if we continue to limit beauty to just one size, one shape, one look, one shade, we're missing it. We're missing so much of nature's treasures, of the beauty within all of us. And how much brighter the world would be if we saw and celebrated all of its beauty, in every shade.

But she also has a few more goals. "These next goals are personal," her mom laughed, knowing what Grace was about to say.

"I really would like to have a boyfriend and I want to get engaged," Grace told me.

"I'm with you, girl!" I laughed. "I don't have a boyfriend, either, so I would like to find him." We all laughed.

"We keep praying for it every night," Linda said, smiling, about a boyfriend. "When she was younger, we made this vision board for her and we put all the things that she wanted on it. But we've never put a boyfriend on there and, now, we're going to put a boyfriend on there."

"Do you have any celebrity crushes?" I asked her.

Oh, yeah!" Grace said. "Zac Efron."

I immediately gushed back at her and said, "Oh, I love him…Grace, you've got to get Zac Efron on your vision board!"

Zac, Grace is ready for you.

*

Grace and Linda have been on quite a journey together, both of them leading with their determination and nothing's-stopping-us attitude. They have and continue to work hard every single day.

But what I loved most about speaking with them is seeing their bond, a mother and daughter who have grown so close, so full of love for each other, so grateful to be learning and growing and discovering together. They continue to explore, treating learning as a life-long adventure.

But, sometimes, girls just wanna have fun and they find little moments to let it all out and be free together. "A lot of times when we're getting ready in the morning," Linda told me, "we'll have music playing. Or if she's getting ready to do a speech, we just start spontaneous dancing first. We just get together and get hyped up. She's a fun, kind of free spirit girl."

"What are your favorites to dance to?" I asked them.

"We love Meghan Trainor and Bruno Mars. We definitely like Justin Timberlake. And we're both Lionel Richie fans and the Bee Gees."

I told them that Brittany and I love to do carpool karaoke or have our own dance parties, and our favorites are Meghan Trainor and Bruno Mars. ("Dear

Future Husband" is our go-to). "So, one day, we're going to have to get together for one big dance party!" I told them.

They both smiled. "Absolutely."

Dance is a celebration; you've got to move with the rhythm of you. And moving with your own rhythm— being who you are and letting it out—there's nothing better.

This is true beauty. Yes, this.

*

True love and compassion is the strongest force in the world, but also the least used and the most ignored. Do not give up hope and do not let the hatred of others drown you. Instead, let it be fuel to the fire of your spirit. Let your light shine bright.

—Robert Henson

*

The privilege of a lifetime is being who you are.

—Joseph Campbell

*

The Dancing Dad

Kenny Clutch is a motivational speaker, a dancer, and Kristian's dad. Kristian happens to have Down syndrome.

In 2017, Kristian entered the world. He was Kenny's fourth child, and his dad describes him as "always loving, always cheerful." Even from the start, he was motivated and a "motivator," Kenny said. "He's not scared of anything. He's just not scared."

There are two things you need to know about his birth, besides that it was, of course, a blessing to the world, one more being brought here to bring something special that only he could bring. We've all got our own purpose and reason for being. Those two things are, one, Kristian was born with Down syndrome. And, two, he spent ten days in the neonatal intensive care unit (or NICU) for a rare blood disorder.

"The doctor told us we had to get his red blood cell count up," Kenny said. And the doctor also said, "At some point in his life, he may develop leukemia."

"Now, I'm a believer," Kenny said, "so I was like, *Nah, we good*," meaning everything was going to be just fine; God wasn't going to let Kristian develop leukemia. "But you never know what's going to happen," Kenny added, "until it really hits home."

*

In March 2018, Kristian got a fever. No big deal; toddlers get fevers. But then another fever came a month later. At that point, Kristian had been going to the hematologist every week to get his blood checked out. He'd get pricked with a needle but, like his dad said, he wasn't scared of anything, so he "took it like a champ" and everything kept going as it had before.

By June 2018, Kristian and his family were on the way to a Family Fun Day of their own making at Dave & Busters. Since Kristian's hematology appointments were nothing unusual, they figured they'd stop there first, Kristian would get his blood checked out, and then they'd head out for their family fun. "But we were in there," Kenny described of that fateful hematologist appointment on June 19, "longer than expected." That one appointment would turn into 32 days in the hospital.

On June 19, Kristian was diagnosed with leukemia, a blood cancer.

"Our whole world flipped upside down in a matter of seconds," Kenny said. "Everything shifted. We didn't go to Dave & Busters that day, or the whole summer."

*

This unexpected turn, a nightmare for any parent, would send Kenny on his own journey, calling on him to look deeper within to see who he truly is, how he wanted to hold space for his family, and how he wanted to share his gifts with the world.

Of course, it didn't begin with that much clarity; when our worlds flip upside down it takes some time to reorient ourselves, to find the grace even in the most devastating circumstances. It began with something as simple as this:

When Kristian was in the hospital, holed up in a room where everyone, as his dad said, "had to be booted and suited" to enter in order to protect his weakened immune system, he received lots of therapies. There were many medical interventions of course, but there were also a few remedies for the soul that were offered to him, something to bring a little joy into a space that felt so dark. One of those therapies was music therapy.

Kristian's dad, Kenny, had grown up dancing. Laughing, he said of that first music therapy session, "Now I'm hip hop, so I'm going to be honest, the ukuleles they brought in weren't cutting it." After suffering through Kristian's first ukulele-filled music therapy session, Kenny knew he could do better. "I was ready to take over the musical therapy part," he said. "Let Dad handle that."

THE DANCING DAD

At the time, Kenny and his wife owned a dance studio. So about eight days into Kristian's time in the hospital when the ukulele music therapy wasn't quite cutting it, Kenny instructed his wife to turn on the music—hip hop this time—and, as he said, "Let's get down for Kristian." Right in the middle of the hospital room, Kenny started dancing to cheer up his son.

*

It was never meant to be bigger than that, more than a dad trying to show his son his love by dancing. They decided to record a few videos of it, just to send to family and friends to document the journey and let them know that everything was okay. As Kenny later described it, "We had to set the atmosphere" inside the hospital and outside it. They wanted Kristian's room to be full of positivity and they wanted even those outside to feel that positivity, too. They wanted to cultivate wellbeing and uplift, not pity.

"So I danced for him," Kenny said. "And next thing you know, Kristian's moving his little arms, his little legs. He's loving it." And he's dancing, too.

The first video they posted online went "a little viral," Kenny said. It got about 10,000 hits. They were in a hospital in Philadelphia at the time, less than an hour from their home in New Jersey, and a Philadelphia-based TV show called *RightThisMinute* called them up and asked to feature their story. "People were loving what we were doing," Kenny said, "so we started doing more."

This is when the shift really started happening. Fast forward to day 32 in the hospital. Kristian's blood count numbers were up, which was good, and Kenny was just trying to keep Kristian, his wife, and his whole family motivated. That's when the doctors walked in and said, "We've got good news; Kristian can go home." He had made enough improvements in those 32 days that it was safe for him to return home. "It was the most exciting day of our life," Kenny said. Kenny explained that, over that past month, it felt like they had practically moved into the hospital, bringing their whole lives with them. So they tried to pack as quickly as possible, excited to move all their stuff out and return to something a little more normal.

On Day 32, something serendipitous also happened. The R&B singer Ciara had just come out with a new song called "Level Up." Kenny's dance studio was called Level Dance Complex, so he thought it was only right that he record another dancing video with Kristian using her "Level Up" song to celebrate this milestone in Kristian's journey. It was the last video they made during that first round of treatments, right before Kristian got discharged. Thinking he was inventing a hashtag, Kenny quickly posted it online and added #LevelUpChallenge. Then they packed up and got out of there.

The thing is Kenny hadn't realized that he didn't start the Level Up Challenge hashtag; Ciara had already started one. At the time he posted the video, Kenny had about five thousand followers on Instagram. Within one hour, his video had 20,000 views. By the time they got home that day, it had been viewed 80,000 times. By the time they went to sleep that night, 100,000 views. And by the next morning, over 800,000 people had viewed it.

The next day, Kenny's wife called him. He didn't answer right away. (He teases now that this would become a reminder to always answer the phone the first time your wife calls you.) The second time she called, he picked up. "Ciara just reposted your video," she said. "For real?" he asked. He couldn't believe it.

But it was true. Ciara reposted it. Halle Berry reposted it. D.L. Hughley. And that's when the media calls began flooding in. He got interview requests from NBC, ABC, CBS, Fox News, the BBC, news stations in Italy, in Canada. "Interview after interview after interview," he said. "And everyone was speaking about 'the dancing dad,'" he said. "Who's the dancing dad?" he asked. "You are," they said. The media were smitten; they had anointed him with their own nickname.

Within one day, Kenny went from having about 5,000 Instagram followers to over 50,000. "This is crazy," he said. They were an overnight sensation.

*

THE DANCING DAD

Long before Kenny started dancing for Kristian in a hospital room in Philadelphia, he started dancing for himself.

"I was born in Newark," he told me, and his family eventually moved to a small town in New Jersey called Willingboro, where he grew up. "I started dancing when I was about 13. I took an interest to it—at parties, school dances. Even in high school, I would always get in the circles or go to different clubs and just dance for fun."

It was always meant to be fun until he was about 19, when he started realizing, *maybe I can do this for a career.* When he was 19, a close friend (who's still a close friend today), told Kenny he was organizing a group, pulling together a group of guys to dance as the opening act for his dad's African drum group. The drum group performed at local events—at the library, community events, schools. "He knew I was a dancer in the neighborhood. So that's how we got started," Kenny said. "And we would be in my house or his house and just be practicing. We didn't have a dance studio or any real training, none of that. We just had the love of dance and we just wanted to be dope hip hop dancers." Kenny said he essentially learned on the job, discovering the different styles of street dance by actually going into the clubs.

When you talk to Kenny about dance, you can feel the passion in his voice. It's one of the reasons I enjoy talking to people about what they love, whether I love that same thing or not: you can feel *it* in them, that excitement, that natural calling, the way they light up. It's an energy, and it's contagious. "What did you love about dancing?" I asked him, wanting to know what drew him to it, what quickened his heartbeat a little when he talked about it.

"I think it was just the rawness of it," he told me, "the purity of hip hop." Dance is visceral, physical, an intimate expression of what's in you. And to be a good dancer, a compelling dancer, you have to be present, really present right here, right now.

Kenny also liked the way dance made him feel. "It made me feel like I was actually good at something," he said. "When you're a teenager, you're kind of trying to figure out what exactly are you good at. For me, I couldn't see myself at 21 or 22 or even 30, to be honest. I'm 36 now. But back then, I didn't know what I wanted to do with my life. I was good at certain things, but I wasn't great at anything. Until dance came along. And it was something I just wanted," he trailed off for a moment. He was drawn to the style of dance, the music, the atmosphere, and "the love that people have for one another when we were dancing in circles." Dance was not only an intimate expression of who he was, it was an expression of community, of connection, of support. Dancing together, he told me, "was how we helped one another through. We weren't doing it for the money or fame. We were just doing it because we loved it. This was our escape. It just happened to turn into something more than that."

Being in hip hop, Kenny said, was not easy. Years later, when Kenny was 34 and his toddler Kristian went into the hospital for leukemia, he focused on positivity, that was his power, his healing gift to his son. But it wasn't always easy being positive when he was a teen and in his early twenties. "Everyday wasn't peachy," he said. "Growing up where I grew up, you had to have some thick skin…People would call you corny, saying *why you dancing like this?* Or *you off-beat*. It was the realest of the real." But on those dance floors, Kenny began to realize something: it's not how life comes at you, it's how you choose to respond. "There's a difference," he told me. "If you react in a negative way, then…it may not turn out the way you planned." There were repercussions, he was saying. "But if you respond in a positive way, not only are you protecting your peace, but you're also showing true leadership and honor…and you're showing that other person that there are other ways to handle that situation. It doesn't necessarily have to end up in something violent…you don't have to escalate the situation."

From dance, he learned the power of holding onto your peace. And, he realized, in every situation that arises in your life, there are two ways to respond: with positivity or with negativity. When Kristian's cancer arose all those years later, put on the spot, Kenny knew which way he was going to respond.

*

"When you're in a negative situation and it hits you, we get impulsive," Kenny said. "We get super emotional, we don't know how to act, we throw our hands up…The reality is we have to deal with it. But *how?* is the question. People say, *Be positive, be positive*, but how? Let's be real here. How do you really be positive when your son is fighting for his life?"

When you're faced as a parent with such an arduous and uncertain medical journey for your child, I imagine you can feel powerless. Kenny wished he could just switch places with Kristian. He couldn't give him medical treatments, couldn't blast the cancer away with his own hands. "That's when your faith is really tested." So he had a talk with God, "just me and Him."

God told him to pray, to join in a circle around his son before the first chemo treatment even hit his body, and just pray. This is when Kenny knew: praying was not merely a plea to God, it was protection and an offering of peace and love. With his family joined in prayer around his son, they were what Kenny would come to call "setting the atmosphere," filling that hospital room with as much love and positivity as they could. Because, for Kenny, healing was not just a physical journey; it was spiritual. We must also honor the soul.

*

When Kenny began to "set the atmosphere" for his son, he made a statement to everyone who was going to be involved with Kristian's treatment, from his family to the doctors to the hospital staff to friends seeking updates and sending prayers from beyond the hospital's walls: "There's no negativity involved." He told the doctors that even if they had to deliver bad news, they had to find a way to bring bad news in a positive way. This was a mind shift, shifting the focus of everyone in the room from negative to positive. Because where your attention goes, your life may flow. "When we change the mind," he told me, "we change the game."

Later, Kenny would describe it to me like this: "Listen, it's like setting the tone. When you walk into a room where everyone's angry, you may be like, *I'm going to be angry, too*, because it may be contagious. But when you walk into a room and everybody has faith, you're going to have faith, too." I immediately thought of those collective experiences we share in big groups: the way we feel inside a concert stadium, how the songs, the energy, the love is somehow heightened. It's why we seek out music together, not always just listening solo on our iPhones. There's an energy that happens when people come together, and Kenny was going to choose to create a very specific energy for his son. So when it came to Kristian's hospital room, Kenny set the tone: "Anyone who walks in this room," he thought, "will know that it's this positive atmosphere…and when you walk in, it's going to be super contagious. You can't walk in here with a negative attitude."

And so it was.

*

When we focus on healing, we often talk about moving towards "the light." We're reminded to "be positive" and "be the light." But sometimes this message gets confused for *only* feeling the light and blocking out everything else. Setting the atmosphere isn't a denial of the realities of life; it's simply a way to see the world. Kenny was inviting everyone around Kristian to see the world through a prism of positivity, to invite a transformative energy into that space so that Kristian could feel it, too, and his soul could be bolstered.

Kenny felt the pressure to be the fire starter of this light, this positivity, trying to lift the energy for his son, his wife, his children. But I wanted to know how he processed his own grief. I wanted to know what he did with those heavy energies, because in healing, we must also see and deal with the darkness.

"You were holding up so much for your family," I said to him. "Did you ever have private moments where you just felt the heaviness?"

"Absolutely. I remember one time—this was maybe day six or seven after Kristian had gotten diagnosed—and I'm going back and forth with my family. I'm getting my children over to their grandma's house. They're sleeping on an air mattress, three of them on an air mattress the entire summer. It wasn't the most comfortable thing in the world. And I'm driving back over to the hospital and there's this heavy storm. Mind you, this is six or seven days after he was diagnosed. I haven't cried a bit. When the storm actually came and I'm driving over the Ben Franklin Bridge, that's when the storm hit in my eyes and that's when everything dropped. It just came out.

"Many times, I've had to hold a lot of things in because I wanted to remain strong. This is something I have to work on, even to this day," he admitted, "learning to be vulnerable, to express myself. And that was one of those moments where I had to just let it go, let it out now, because if you don't let it out, this thing is just going to build and build and build, and it's not going to be safe for my son, it's not going to be safe for my family or anybody. So I knew: *Kenny, you have to let this out now because you have a long journey ahead of you.*"

Kenny described it like going on a long road trip: "You've gotta gas up," he said. "You've gotta get everything ready for that long road trip before you go on that trip. You've got to check the oil, you've got to make sure the transmission is right, the tires are right —you've got to make sure every nook and cranny of the car is good because if you're going across country, you don't want a breakdown halfway through when you're in Chicago. So it's good to get all the dirt and the gook out now before you make this long, long journey."

In other words, you've got to feel the grief or the sadness or the worry—whatever is moving through your body—and you've got to let it out. Once you've felt it fully, you can begin to release it and you can begin to see your journey ahead through a new lens. This is not easy. But, for Kenny, this was the only way.

*

Happiness is the consequence of personal effort. You fight for it, strive for it, insist upon it, and sometimes even travel around the world looking for it. You have to participate relentlessly in the manifestations of your own blessings.

—Elizabeth Gilbert

*

From watching videos of Kenny dancing with Kristian, I can assure you they are magnetic. I dare you not to smile as you watch. But I wanted to know what Kenny thought about their unexpected catchiness—"What do you think made your videos go viral?" I asked him.

"I think what's so catchy about it," he said, "is that you see a father dancing with his son. You see a father caring for his family. You see a father just being an ordinary person, just coming out and being a father." In other words, people were attracted to the love, to something so simple as a father showing up, being vulnerable, being loving, trying to do everything he can for his son. We're drawn to love.

But perhaps it was deeper than that. "So many times in life," Kenny said, "especially for black fathers, we get this persona that we're not there for our children. So I think it's important to show that there are guys who are out there—not just black fathers but fathers of all ethnicities—we're out here and we're doing for our kids, for our sons and daughters." Kenny was not an absent dad; he was not only present in body but in spirit. He was offering his son the deep gift of seeing him, holding space for him, of giving him his time, his presence, his energy.

And Kenny dancing with Kristian was also a gift of hope. Not only to Kristian but, as it turned out, to the whole world, to all of us who are blessed to get to see the magic of their dancing ourselves. "With so much negativity going on, it's good to see some rain of positivity come down." This is important, Kenny insisted, "because the imagery of what we see in life can ultimately dictate and feed our spirit and our soul to where we actually start to act like that if we see it too much." In other words, the more negativity we take in, the more our attention flows to negativity, the more we embody it and, perhaps, begin to live it out, to act on it. "So it's important that people like myself," Kenny said, "we fill up the social media feed [and the world] with positivity. To show people— there's hope in the world. Be a beacon of hope." Rather than negativity, Kenny says, "We can show you there's something different out here."

Kenny started dancing in the hospital to cheer up his son and, as he said, "to keep his family sane" during a very insane time in their lives. "But when I saw that people were attracted to it, and they're like, *this just made my day*, I heard the call: start helping other people on another level by doing this," he heard—by spreading positivity.

*

This year, Kenny has embarked on bringing this call, his call, to the world in a bigger way. He's launched Shift Makers, an organization on a mission to help you shift your life—to help you set your atmosphere, build what he calls your "pillars of strength," and to discover your gifts—and to use your gift to make a shift. He's got a podcast, a YouTube channel, and an ever-growing Instagram following.

"I don't ever want to say Kristian's cancer happened for a reason or that it was meant to be. It wasn't," I said to Kenny. "But you've talked about 'getting it,' having that moment where everything clicked in, when you saw clearly why this positivity you began putting out in the world really matters. Do you feel like what Kristian's journey has led to—you sharing your wisdom and being a speaker and you and Kristian just sharing your positivity—was that destiny always waiting for you?"

"I believe it was, to be honest," Kenny said. And then, laughing, he added, "I didn't know it though. I really didn't know it. You could have fooled me."

Kenny said that if I were to tell him, 17 years ago, that this was his future, he wouldn't have believed it. "Don't play with my emotions like that," he teased. "I thought I was supposed to be dancing on stage with Beyoncé or something like that, doing shows with some of the biggest hip hop and R&B stars, and if you told me I was going to be some motivational speaker and that my son was going to be inspiring millions of people across the world, I would have thought you were lying."

When the doctors first diagnosed Kristian with leukemia, they told Kenny and his family that this journey was going to be about 300 days long. But Kristian's recovery time was cut in half: in just 149 days, he was in remission. "The doctors couldn't believe it was cut that short," Kenny said. He attributes this to Kristian's fighting spirit, to the positive atmosphere they created, to the doctors, and to God's guidance. And, to Kenny, this miraculously quick recovery was also a sign: hidden within that journey he never wished for was also his and his son's gifts: they were going to uplift the world.

So, yes, yes, this was destiny. Not the cancer, but the love and the hope the two of them, father and son, have built and unleashed together.

*

*I want to think again of
dangerous and noble things.
I want to be light and
frolicsome. I want to be
improbable beautiful and
afraid of nothing,
as though I had wings.*

—Mary Oliver

*

I think so many of us struggle sometimes to accept our purpose or to accept the way life is unfolding for us. Perhaps we've imagined another path in our heads and when things don't go our way, we get angry or we question what we're experiencing. We think that what's being brought to us is wrong, that we're missing our true destiny.

But this journey has taught Kenny to accept his purpose, even if it doesn't look like what he once thought. Talking about his unanticipated purpose, he said, "The thing is, I've accepted it. I've accepted it. No, I'm not dancing with the biggest stars in the world. I'm dancing for something that's much greater. I'm dancing for people, [the people] that make this world. I'm dancing for the people that need me in this world. They don't need another entertainer. They need someone who's going to speak life, who's going to be a beacon of hope…They need someone who's going to…support them in fulfilling their own dreams in life.

"So, no, it's not about just dancing and going on stage and seeing 30,000 people scream for whatever reason. No, every person in this world has something going on with them and every single person has a purpose. So…it is my duty while I'm here to fulfill my purpose and push others to fulfill theirs because we've all got work to do."

"Mmm," I said, "yes."

*

We must be willing to let go of the life we planned so as to have the life that is waiting for us.

—Joseph Campbell

*

What I appreciate about Kenny's mission is he's not trying to uplift others by pretending he's some superhuman figure. He's showing the world that his attitude is possible for everyone, that his mind-shift turned life-shift is within their reach, too.

When I asked Kenny what it has felt like to step into the spotlight, to be seen and heard in such a public way, he told me, "It's been pretty cool, I guess." But he insisted he's "stayed grounded…I put God before everything," he told me. "And I move and leap with how God moves. Period."

"At the end of the day," he said, "I'm a father. I'm a husband. I've got kids to feed, I've got real issues going on, too. I want people to understand that. Yeah, I'm pretty popular on Instagram and TikTok. Yeah, that's cool. But I'm a real person. I'm a human being. I pay my bills just like you. I put on my pants, just like you. I'm an ordinary person with an extraordinary way of thinking."

And you can be, too. Kenny shows you that he's here with you, he's like you, he's human—and you're not alone.

Kenny also insists that this new platform of his comes with responsibility. He values the community around him, the ones who have made his work possible. So when people send him private messages on social media asking for hope, he insists that he wants to try to answer them; he's not too busy for them or above them. "So why not respond to these people?" he said. "At the end of the day, we're all brothers and sisters here on Earth. That's how I look at it. Why not help?

"The Bible says, 'Love thy neighbor as thyself,' so I'm going to live by that." He describes a woman who reached out and said, "I've got six months to live, what do I do?" Or the person who said, "My mom is going through her pacemaker—they took her pacemaker out and she's got seven months left to live. I don't know what to do. I don't know how to move. How am I supposed to get through this. Your story inspires me, Kenny. What did you do?"

Kenny is committed to giving them exactly what he did, setting the atmosphere, building his pillars of strength. "Sometimes, one minute on Instagram is not going to cut it. Sometimes, you actually have to go deeper with people," he acknowledged. But as often as he can, he's going to try. "Because, if not, who knows [what happens] when we get to the other side. I don't want to be the one who [at the end of his life] is like, 'Oh, I missed all these [messages],' and it's like, 'Well, that was part of your destiny. You were supposed to serve that person and you didn't because you got caught up in the lights and all the action, thinking that you're too good.' I am not too good," he insisted. "I am exactly who God created me to be, and I'm supposed to connect with people and help them the best way I can while I'm here."

*

we all together—
fireflies
in the night
dreaming up
the cosmos

—Francisco X. Alarcón

*

There was still one part of this journey we hadn't talked much about: Kristian has Down syndrome. So Kenny is sharing his dancing journey with Kristian not only as a father bringing hope and positivity to the world, but as a father of a child with Down syndrome.

Because I am the Social Media Director of Brittany's Baskets of Hope, I spend a lot of time scrolling through sweet baby photos of children with Down syndrome. Often, these accounts are managed by the babies' moms. It requires far more digging to find accounts run by fathers, especially fathers (or mothers) of color. This doesn't mean these fathers are not very present in their children's lives, just that perhaps they don't choose to share their child's journey in the same way or perhaps there are additional barriers to being seen. Either way, the result is that we don't see fathers represented as fully on social media as we do many women. So I wanted to know why representation—in this case, of fathers and their children with Down syndrome—on social media matters to Kenny. Why is it so important for him to share his story?

"I think it's needed," Kenny said. "I think the Down syndrome community needs a voice. And there are many women that have that voice, but not enough men have that voice for their children."

Kenny went on to explain something I hadn't considered before, that perhaps there's some shame for men around having a child with special needs. "I also believe [that telling our story] is about showing unconditional love for the condition of your child," he told me. "At the end of the day, you were given a child, no matter their condition. And there are some people that don't get that blessing. There are certain people in life that don't, so why be ashamed? Why hide the fact that you're a dad? Yeah, your son or daughter has Down syndrome or some sort of special need. So? At the end of the day, they're human beings. They're just different. We're all different. There are over 7 billion people that live on this planet, and we've all got a different fingerprint. So nobody is really the same at the end of the day. Why not treat them as such?"

I believe Kenny was speaking to an unnamed shame that some fathers, as what he called "the leaders of their families" may feel when they have a child with different abilities. It's as if, sometimes, they feel like or they're made to feel like this is a failing on their part, like perhaps that means they're not man enough, like they did something wrong. Kenny told me that if men are not showing up as present and grateful fathers to their children, no matter who they are or how they're born, "What are we doing? What is this all about? It just bothers me sometimes when I get these stories of fathers that are not there for their children that have a special need. Or when they're saying that [they] can't make children like that," like, again, having a child with Down syndrome is some sort of failing on their part, a reflection of their lack of manhood.

"We have no control over whether we're going to have a boy or a girl or whether they're going to have Trisomy 21 or not. We don't control that. All we do is make it happen…I feel like there's just so much misconception around the Down syndrome community, around what they can't do, that they're never going to be able to do this, and doctors saying you should abort." This is why Kenny wants to be part of the movement of fathers with a child with Down syndrome showing the truth. That all children have value and that showing up as a father, being seen as vulnerable and present and caring with your children, no matter who they are, matters.

"I just feel, in my body and my soul and my spirit, it's time for someone to step up and say something. Because the Bible says, 'Speak for those who cannot speak for themselves.'" So if Kristian, at three years old, can't quite advocate for himself yet, Kenny wants to be there for him. If he can't speak for himself, Kenny said, "well, guess what, I can. I'm going to say something. I'm going to continue to always advocate for [him] and always be [his] biggest supporter because [people with Down syndrome] can do anything and everything that anyone else can.

"Let's start educating people on what type of special beings these people absolutely are," Kenny went on. "I'm always going to make sure that I'm here to uplift and to elevate and to stand firm."

*

At the end of our conversation, I asked Kenny more specifically about being a father. "Finish the sentence," I told him. "The best part of being a father is…"

"The best part of being a father is…oh, man!" he laughed. "The best part of being a father is getting to learn every day about these four different personalities that I have living in my house," he said referring to his four kids, three boys and a girl. "And learning to try to navigate each of them and point them in the right direction. Being a father is a learning experience. It's something I wouldn't trade for the world."

Kenny told me that when he was a kid he didn't often look forward, unsure of where he'd be in five years, in ten years, in twenty, but he did always have aspirations of being a dad. "My aspirations to be a dad and a husband were there at an early age," he said. And he first became a dad relatively young, at 21. Things kind of "veered off" from there, he told me, regarding his certainty of what his purpose was and his role as a father, though he was always very present. But he has come back to knowing who he is and what his role is in a strong way, and father is at the top and center of his list.

As a father, Kenny is particularly thrilled about this: Kristian has officially been cancer-free for 21 months, a glorious milestone. "So what does Kristian love to do now that he's out of the hospital and feeling healthy, again?" I asked him.

Kristian just learned to walk a few months ago, so Kenny said, he loves to "run everywhere! If you put this boy down, it's over…he's a loose goose."

"It sounds like he's unstoppable now that he's learned to walk," I told Kenny.

He laughed and agreed.

Kenny also told me Kristian "loves dancing, of course. And watching Alvin and the Chipmunks. That's his morning cartoon that he watches every morning and he's glued to it."

"Okay, last one," I told Kenny. "Finish the sentence: Kristian is…"

"Hah!" Kenny laughed, delighted by trying to put all that his son is into a few words. "A warrior," he proclaimed. "He is a motivator without even speaking words. You want to talk about actions speaking louder than words? He is that. He doesn't just speak it; he is it."

Out of this test of faith, Kenny and Kristian have seen clearly and stepped into their gifts, Kristian as a warrior, a joy, a toddler troublemaker sometimes, an unstoppable force, and Kenny as a motivator, a speaker, a preacher of "the shift."

Out of all the pain, Kenny told me, all the darkness, when you look to the positive, "somewhere in there is your gift. Is your purpose. We use that gift to make the shift in our lives. I used my gift to help my son defeat cancer."

And now he's inviting all of us to use our gifts, too.

"The question is: do you want it?" he asked. "Do you really want change?"

If you lean in to the positivity, Kenny insists, "you can reign."

It's up to you. When your purpose comes knocking, will you answer the door?

*

*Hard times require
furious dancing.
Each of us is proof.*

—Alice Walker

*

The Grateful Friend

I am Brittany Schiavone's grateful friend.
Brittany Schiavone is the founder of Brittany's Baskets of
Hope, a 501(c)3 nonprofit organization on a mission to spread
resources, hope, and love to families of new babies with
Down syndrome across the country by delivering
welcome baskets of hope to them.
Brittany happens to have Down syndrome.

I serve on the Board of Directors of her organization.

I walked into Brittany's kitchen the other morning. I
was there for one of our "packing parties," where we
gather friends and family together to celebrate our
latest basket of hope recipients and hand-pack each
basket uniquely for each family of a new baby with
Down syndrome. Brittany was finishing up her
breakfast—her mom had made pancakes—and
Brittany just said to me, "So when is it?"

I was almost 100% certain of what she was referring
to when she said, "it," but I thought to myself, "Who
am I to assume?" So I asked her, just in case, "When
is what?"

She looked at me and let out a sigh, "You know," she
said, as if saying with her gestures, "Come on, you
know you know what I'm thinking."

"Our Friendiversary?" I asked her, referring to the name we've given to our friendship anniversary, when we celebrate how long we've known each other.

"Of course," she said.

"Not for another six months," I told her, "in November. I think it'll be six years!"

*

Brittany and I met on a cool November morning in 2014. As Brittany always says, "We met at the church."

A few weeks earlier, a mutual friend, Theresa, had told me, "I have a friend, Brittany, and I think you would just love her." Around that time, I had just started my own organic skincare business and Theresa told me, "She's an entrepreneur, too." Brittany had just launched her own social enterprise, her 501(c)3 nonprofit, Brittany's Baskets of Hope.

The next morning after Theresa mentioned Brittany, I was still thinking about her, this mystery girl who was using her gifts to support families that began just like hers, with new babies with Down syndrome. In a few weeks, I would be hosting a small talk about wellbeing and the earth in a local church basement. I wasn't sure what I was going to do about admission, but in that moment, I knew. I decided that, rather than collect a ticket cost for entry, I was going to invite guests to make a donation, if they wished, to Brittany's Baskets of Hope. I looked up Brittany's organization online, found an email address, and sent a message: *Would you like to come to the talk and speak for a few minutes at the beginning,* I asked her, *to introduce the guests to your mission?*

To my delight, she agreed, and that was that.

So on that cool November Saturday in 2014, as I prepared the church basement with a few rows of chairs, Brittany walked in with her mom and her support staff, Ali, carrying a big basket full of bundles of gifts, resources, and love. I invited her to put it down on the table I had set up as her makeshift display and then I gave her a hug, introducing myself.

To this day, we still tease that from that first hug, we knew: we were going to be friends.

At the time, Brittany was 25 (I'm one year younger), and I remember beginning my talk after she had spoken, still awed by her. I said something like, "At 25, it's so rare that we know our purpose in life. And, even if we do, that we know how and are ready to act on it. But here Brittany is, at 25 years old, knowing and living her purpose with heart. That's impressive."

It still is.

*

When Brittany graduated from high school, she joined a group day program for adults with different abilities. She was living at home with her parents, but would go the program five days a week. There are probably many adults who love this, the camaraderie, the collective experience, just getting to go with the flow of whatever the day's activities are. But not Brittany.

No, Brittany has always had a fiery independent side (which is what I love about her), so if she was at the day program and they were split into two groups, and one group was assigned to go to the mall and the other to the movies, and she was in the mall group but wanted to go to the movies, she wasn't happy about it. She was a grown woman, she knew what she wanted, and she wanted to direct her own life: to choose what she was going to make of each of her days.

After expressing this to her parents, her mom, Sue, knew they had to make a change. But what?

Eventually, they chose self-direction, a program that allowed Brittany to set her own goals, hire her own staff (formally known as "direct support professionals), and live each day uniquely, as she wanted. These direct support professionals, or DSPs, were often young women around Brittany's age who would help her direct her day and live out her goals.

Before they were hired—and Brittany always teases, "I'm the boss," when we talk about the way she gets to hire her staff—they would go through a vetting process. Brittany and her parents would invite each woman over to her house for a conversation. Once they got the thumbs up from mom and dad, Brittany would get final approval, often inviting the DSP out for some one-on-one time over ice cream. If Brittany approved, the DSP was in. Over the years, as many of these young women have transitioned out of their roles as DSPs and into other jobs and careers, they have remained friends with Brittany because Brittany's just that kind of woman—we all adore her and want to catch up over drinks when we can.

After I met Brittany in that church basement, this is how I stayed in what we refer to as her "circle." I was hired by my boss, Brittany, to be one of her DSPs, where we would focus on her goal of feeling healthy and eating well. (Of the many projects I've embarked on in my life, one of them is studying to become a wellness coach. So I'd be relying on that old trick in my bag to support Brittany in living her fullest, most vital life.)

As we got to work, I introduced Brittany to green smoothies—smoothies whipped up with spinach in the mix. "It sounds gross, I know," I told her, "but I promise we can make it taste good!" After bonding over our mutual love of mangoes, we threw some mangoes and strawberries in there with the spinach and guess what? It was pretty juicy and good. We drank up.

We baked a lot, too, trying to find slightly healthier alternatives to traditional baked delights like brownies (in that recipe experiment, we subbed flour for black beans). Surprisingly, it was pretty yummy. But we definitely had some misses—the zucchini muffins were *not* a hit and Brittany kindly said, "You can take those home, if you want," offering for me to bring them to my grandma, instead.

We went on walks and joined a group of friends on Tuesday mornings in the winter in the mall, doing our mall walking before the stores officially opened. We rolled out yoga mats and did some downward facing dogs (although, mostly, I turned on Bruno Mars and we just danced!). We went to the gym at the local YMCA and walked alongside each other on treadmills. When I would try to pick up the pace on my treadmill, always racing against myself, Brittany would look calm and content and remind me, "Ashley, you don't have to go so fast." And I would smile and tease her, "But I'm going to win." She'd roll her eyes and say, "Oh, you," but we'd both smile because we knew each other so well and as different as we were, we loved each other for it.

Eventually, I would break the news to Brittany and her family that it was time for me to leave their official circle and join the informal one, moving on from being a DSP to other endeavors in my life as my own business grew. "But we're still friends," I promised Brittany. "Always."

But just before I could get my feet out the door, Brittany and her parents had another idea. It was the spring of 2016, and Brittany's nonprofit had been officially launched but not quite moved into action yet. Would I want to join the organization's Board of Directors and help officially get it off the ground?

While I knew I was leaving being a DSP to focus on my own endeavors, I felt in my heart this wasn't an opportunity to pass up. Something in me felt lit up by the idea, and by getting to officially remain part of Brittany's circle. A few weeks later, I was in.

*

THE GRATEFUL FRIEND

A few months later, in October 2016—Down
Syndrome Awareness Month—we sent our first
basket of hope to a family in Colorado that had
adopted a little boy, Abel, with Down syndrome. We
filled that first basket, and all our baskets to come,
with resources, with Brittany's story in her own words
and from her parents' perspective. We included the
beloved "Welcome to Holland" poem, a gentle
reminder to parents written in metaphor. The poem
goes along the lines of this: when you found out you
were expecting a child, maybe you were full of
wonder and excitement. Maybe you'd always been
waiting for this moment. And perhaps it was like the
experience of planning your dream trip to Italy. You
imagined it all, were ready to visit the gondolas in
Venice. You wanted to take in all of Italy's beauty. But
when you realized your little bundle of joy happened
to have an extra chromosome—Down syndrome—
it's like your trip was re-routed, this time to Holland.
Holland is not what you planned and, at first, you may
be skeptical: there are no famous gondolas in
Holland. But Holland is also lovely. The pace in
Holland may be a little slower than in Italy, maybe
Holland is a little less flashy. But did you know there
are tulips in spring in Holland? There are windmills in
Holland and Rembrandts, even.

Holland wasn't what you expected, but you've
realized: you've fallen in love with it, too, and
wouldn't want it any other way.

Adding that poem to our baskets is our loving welcome and small burst of hope—just because this is not what you planned, it doesn't mean the road ahead isn't full of beauty. After all, we're the ones who know: Brittany is living proof.

We also included in that first basket and all our baskets little gifts for the baby: there's our signature "Down Right Perfect" onesie, baby blankets handmade by individual knitters and crocheters who donate their time and their creations to us from all across the country. There are children's books (our favorites are by author Nancy Tillman, books that celebrate the arrival of every child in the world, no matter who they are or how they're born. We've even connected with Nancy personally, who has a granddaughter with Down syndrome and who has donated big boxes of her books to us). There are onesies and shimmering golden booties and floral headbands for the girls donated from our friends at Urban Baby Co., and bibs in the shape of animals handmade by our friend Summer in Pennsylvania. Every basket is a little different, tailored to each baby and their family.

To be honest, the plan was never to replace actual baskets with packing boxes and send these gifts of hope to families across the country; it was always meant to be local. But when this seed that Brittany had planted suddenly took off and media attention began rolling in, we went with it and embraced a whole new world.

As I write this to you not quite four years after we sent our first basket of hope, we've now sent over 1,000 baskets to families in all 50 states across the country.

Yes, welcome to Holland, indeed.

*

When I say Brittany planted the seed of this idea, I mean it. But maybe it was also planted in her, something brewing in her since the beginning; maybe this was always her destiny. I like to imagine it was.

Either way, it stemmed from and continues to be driven by her vision and her passion. In fact, not only is she the Founder of Brittany's Baskets of Hope, but I've dubbed her the "Visionary in Chief."

In 2014, a few months before I met her, Brittany was at work at a clothing boutique. On her break, her boss showed her a video about people welcoming new babies to the world. This sparked that seed in Brittany. She came home from work that day and told her parents, "I want to help moms and dads of babies with Down syndrome. I want to give them hope."

Brittany's parents thought this was a lovely and kind idea, but what were they going to do about it? How do you actually give parents hope? So that was that— a nice idea.

But Brittany was persistent or, as I like to say, determined. Over and over again, she reminded her parents: "I want to give new parents hope." Brittany is blessed to have a strong support team around her, including her formal and informal circles. With the help of her parents and her whole team, they did just what Brittany had sought in her life when she left the day program: they helped her direct her goals and her life. Eventually, Brittany's Baskets of Hope, an official 501(c)3 nonprofit, was formed.

*

If you were to ask me now, I would tell you that
working for Brittany's Baskets of Hope has moved
me. Every day, I'm blessed to receive messages from
parents and families across the country with new
babies with Down syndrome. (The best part is that I
also get sent photos of these babies all the time. My
email inbox is more than a to-do list; it's a space of
joy.) And not only that, but I have come to learn what
so many of us learn when we enter Holland instead
of Italy as parents or siblings or friends, when we
become what has been dubbed "the lucky few": the
Down syndrome community is almost unimaginably
loving, creating this huge network of support,
connecting each of us lucky ones locally and globally.

Each day, I post some of those precious baby photos
on our Brittany's Baskets of Hope social media pages
and, each day, people from across the globe comment
on those photos. Often, without ever meeting that
child or that family, they still choose to send an
uplifting message: "Set your sights high," they'll say to
the baby, "You can achieve anything." Or "your smile
brightened my day," or they'll tell stories of their own
children with Down syndrome, who are now grown,
and they'll remind these new parents, these new
inductees to Holland, that this will be a beautiful and
surprising and full journey, with peaks and valleys and
more peaks, just like it is with any other child. Yes,
our whole community rallies together to spread hope.
To me, it feels like each of these comments are

saying, "I see you." "I'm rooting for you." "You are not alone."

But the most surprising part of this journey for me has not just been the love I've gotten to feel and see, not just the families from all over the world I've gotten to connect with and learn from and be inspired by. No, the most surprising part—and the best part—of this journey has been my friendship with Brittany.

When I say that now, I shake my head, wondering how I was surprised by this, how I never anticipated that Brittany's place in my life could delight me and move me and make me laugh and feel, well, like the fullest of friendships. But it did, it surprised me. Today, I know better: friendship comes in all forms, and it's often the friendships that are most unexpected that change you the most because they come with that little extra magic—they catch you off-guard.

*

Each friend represents a world in us, a world possibly not born until they arrive, and it is only by this meeting that a new world is born.

—Anaïs Nin

*

Last year, Brittany and I pre-recorded a video for an event where we were being honored, and the task given to us was to talk about our work and our friendship. We were receiving the award from an organization close to our hearts, from Brittany's broker Barbara, who helps organize Brittany's—and many others'—self-direction support services.

In the video, Brittany and I are sitting next to each other, facing the camera. I'm talking to her as I also talk to the camera. "This next question," I tell Brittany and the camera, "is from Barbara. Barbara said…"

Before I can finish the sentence, Brittany, who adores Barbara and even works in her office once a week, helping with administrative tasks, jumps in playfully, "What did she say?"

I laugh. "Barbara wants to know what you like about me."

Brittany smiles and puts her hand to her heart before saying, "Ashley is a great person, she really supports me…I love her so much and dearly, how much I really care about her." Brittany goes on to talk about how she and I "eat healthy" together, how we bake together and make smoothies and go out to dinner. (Luckily, she does not mention the zucchini muffin mishap when she talks about what we've baked.)

"Ashley's an amazing young girl," Brittany says, and I laugh at the young part. I tease that she's my main PR person, so of course she mentions my organic skincare line (my own personal business), giving my work a shoutout, telling the camera that "Ashley talks about the earth," which is true. I'm always going on about protecting the planet and Brittany graciously puts up with it.

She finishes with, "I love her from inside my heart."

I'm touched by the way she gushed about me, and I put my hand to my heart, feeling it.

"This next question wasn't asked," I say, "but I'm going to answer it anyway. What I love about Brittany…"

Brittany, excited by this, jumps in, "Yeah!"

"I love what an amazing friend you are," I say, turning away from the camera to look at her. "What I love is that you check in on me and you ask if I'm okay. Or you send me heart emojis or your favorite emoji with—" and then we both simultaneously say, "sunglasses."

"I love that you really care about how I'm doing. I love the hugs I get from you."

"Always, always," Brittany says. "If I walk in the room, I give her a hug."

"I get special hugs," I say, confirming it to the camera. "I think my other favorite thing about Brittany. Well, I guess there are a few things. One, that…"

"We're boy crazy!" Brittany exclaims, finishing the sentence for me.

Knowing that this video was going to be played at a special evening event with other support brokers and staff and parents, I laugh, caught-off-guard once again by Brittany, and say, "Okay, I was going to say something way more professional." Still laughing, I turn back to Brittany and say, "So you said we're boy crazy. I was going to say what I love about you is that you live your purpose and you're passionate and you're creative, and I think that's so amazing."

"Yeah," Brittany agrees.

"But, yes," I concede, smiling, "we sing in the car and do carpool karaoke."

"Oh, my gosh, we always do!" Brittany says excitedly.

"And we sing 'Dear Future Husband,'" I add, referencing the Meghan Trainor song that sings like a love letter to her imagined future spouse.

"Yes!" Brittany jumps in, clarifying that the song is "about boys."

*

Brittany and I are both currently single, and we both hope to find a boyfriend someday. Although I always tease her, "But we are strong, independent women… we don't need a man!" As much as we sing about boys —and talk about boys—I also want to affirm that we are enough, just as we are.

But, sometimes, we just can't help ourselves and boys are the topic at hand. And when it comes to men, we do have one thing in common, and that one thing is Derek Hough.

If you don't know, Derek Hough is the *Dancing with the Stars* pro turned *World of Dance* judge with blond hair, blue eyes, and *great* moves.

To be honest, I don't watch his shows anymore. "It hurts my heart too much to see him and not have him," I tease Brittany. But when either of us catches a video clip of him online, we immediately send it to each other. I may try to hide it and say I've grown up, but we're both still kind of smitten.

Last summer, I wasn't single, though. I had a boyfriend. A boyfriend who, unfortunately, was living in another city. So as I hopped off a plane at JFK International Airport outside New York City on my way back from visiting him, I was by myself, lugging my old suitcase from the farthest gate in the airport (and JFK is a big airport) to the exit. I didn't yet have one of those fancy suitcases—and, by fancy, I just mean one that was made within the last decade—that rolled in all sorts of directions effortlessly, wheels turning with ease. I had inherited my grandma's old suitcase, with this very outdated floral pattern on it, and that was what I was using.

So I walked through that airport, lugging my suitcase behind me, looking down at the ground, just ready to finally get home.

I was halfway through the airport when I had that feeling—you know the one, when you feel like there are eyes on you. Again, I had been minding my own business, wrapped up in my own world, my visit with my boyfriend playing through my head, letting a few small but lingering doubts about our relationship pop up in my mind. But in that moment, I felt eyes on me so, without thinking, I looked up. And looking right back at me was Derek Hough.

The Derek Hough.

When he noticed me noticing him, he smiled. To be honest, I don't even know if I smiled back, too caught off guard by his sudden presence in New York (if I had my facts correct, I thought he lived somewhere in LA). He held that smile for a few moments, looking directly at me, and then kept walking right on by, coolly and casually. I stopped, in the middle of the busy airport with people swirling around me in all directions, and looked behind me to confirm: *yes, that was really him.*

As soon as I got outside the airport, I checked his Instagram (you know, as women who are *not* smitten with celebrities they think they've just seen in an airport do). Sure enough, he had just been in New York for a trip. He must have been heading back to LA.

There are three things to do in this instance, when you spot the celebrity crush you have been talking about for five years—and then pretending not to talk about. First, you can let it be and move on with your day and just go home. Second, you can call your boyfriend and tell him how much you love him and miss him already. Or you can go with option three: you can call your girl friend and dish about it.

I chose option three.

While waiting in the chaotic arrivals circle for my ride home, I immediately picked up the phone and called Brittany. "Oh, my gosh," I said, "I just saw Derek Hough!"

We both screamed.

*

Knowing Brittany has been an adventure. Together, we have been on TV shows and podcasts to talk about our work. We've done photoshoots where her natural confidence and what I call her "Beyoncé moves" remind me to let my beauty fly, too, just as it is. We've gotten put up in a fancy Park Avenue hotel by L'Oreal Paris for a Women of Worth gala honoring Brittany herself. (Talk about beauty, inside and out!) We've met celebrities and learned what a red carpet "step and repeat" is when Brittany actually had to walk a red carpet herself. And, most importantly, we've met families all across the country who just happen to be raising a little one with Down syndrome. This has changed us and, I assure you, made us better. One of the other things I love about Brittany is the way she has grown me, the ways I have learned about myself from her.

But the most rewarding adventure has been getting to know her and her whole family. I tease that her mom, Sue, is my second mom and that her dad, Rocky, is my second dad. They've gotten to know my whole family, too, and even our parents have become friends, texting each other and going out to dinner from time to time.

When I thought about writing this book, I knew I wanted to include Brittany's story in some way. And, at first, I thought I'd just give you the facts of her life ——one more woman with Down syndrome who is leading the way, reminding all of us that we have purpose, we have value, and if we follow our hearts, we just may change the world. But as the Social Media Director and whatever-we-need-behind-the-scenes person at Brittany's Baskets of Hope, I spend most of my days telling Brittany's story in some way.

And, I realized, I didn't want to tell just one more story of a successful and thriving woman with Down syndrome. Because, truthfully, there are so many of them. Brittany is not alone and that's what's so important to emphasize. Brittany is not some aberration, a rare case of a woman with Down syndrome defying the odds. They all are because, like the rest of us, they were all born for a reason, with a unique gift to give the world. As Brittany always says, "People with Down syndrome can do anything— really, really anything."

So I was almost going to leave Brittany's story out. I was almost going to just mention it in the introduction and move on. Not because I don't love her and adore her and think she's a game changer, but because something about it felt like it had already been told in the pages of this book.

But as I searched for one last story to tell in this book, sending out a message on social media calling on the Down syndrome community to submit their stories to me for consideration, I realized the one story that was missing wasn't out there, it was in here.

It wasn't Brittany's story I had to tell; it was ours. The story of our friendship.

This book wouldn't be without her. So many of the greatest adventures and so much of the joy of my life would never have happened.

Brittany, you make me better. I am so lucky to call you my friend.

In just the way you love me, I love you—from inside my heart. Always.

*

*You are a magnificent creature.
Start knowing it.*

—Elizabeth Gilbert

*

Gratitude for the Cover Photo

The Down Right Perfect cutie on the cover of this book is Brooks Charlson. He was photographed by his mom, Maddy Charlson.

I asked Maddy to tell me more about her son, and she said,

"Brooks decided to come into this world being extra special. He has shown not only us but everyone around him the true meaning of love.
He has changed the lives of so many people, we cannot wait to see him change the lives of many more!"

A Note on the Quotes

On page 87, I've shared the words of
Mikey Berryman.

On page 119, I've shared the words of
Robert Henson.

Both men wrote these words in letters to me from
inside a Virginia state prison, where they both are
currently incarcerated.

Through years of exchanges for another book I wrote
called *I Have Waited for You*, these men have shown me
the power of friendship, of transformation, of faith,
and of hope.

About the Author

Ashley Asti is a writer, advocate, and entrepreneur who intertwines her commitment to authenticity throughout all aspects of her life. She is a prolific author, a Board Member of the nonprofit Brittany's Baskets of Hope, and she has embraced her passion for yoga by becoming a certified instructor. She is also the creator of an organic skincare line designed to honor our bodies, our planet, and our spirits.

Her mission in all her work is to connect her students, readers, and all those who cross her path to the beauty of their souls.

ashleyasti.com

 @ashley_asti   @ashleyasti

Made in the USA
Coppell, TX
13 October 2020

39733299R10108